INNOVATIONS IN EDUCATION SERIES

Edited by Robert J. Brown

1. Edward J. Dirkswager, editor. *Teachers as Owners: A Key to Revitalizing Public Education.* 2002.
2. Darlene Leiding. *The Won't Learners: An Answer to Their Cry.* 2002.
3. Ronald J. Newell. *Passion for Learning: How a Project-Based System Meets the Needs of High School Students in the 21st Century.* 2003.
4. Sarah J. Noonan. *The Elements of Leadership: What You Should Know.* 2003.
5. Jeffrey R. Cornwall. *From the Ground Up: Entrepreneurial School Leadership.* 2003.
6. Linda Schaak Distad and Joan Cady Brownstein. *Talking Teaching: Implementing Reflective Practice in Groups.* 2004.
7. Darlene Leiding. *Managers Make the Difference: Managing vs. Leading in Our Schools.* 2004.
8. Darlene Leiding: *Racial Bias in the Classroom: Can Teachers Reach All Children?* 2006.
9. Tim R. McDonald. *UNSUSTAINABLE: A Strategy for Making Public Schooling More Productive, Effective, and Affordable.* 2010.

UNSUSTAINABLE

A Strategy for Making Public Schooling More Productive, Effective, and Affordable

Tim R. McDonald

Innovations in Education Series, No. 9

ROWMAN & LITTLEFIELD EDUCATION

A division of
ROWMAN & LITTLEFIELD PUBLISHERS, INC.
Lanham • Boulder • New York • Toronto • Plymouth, UK

Published in the United States of America
by Rowman & Littlefield Publishers, Inc.
A wholly owned subsidiary of
The Rowman & Littlefield Publishing Group, Inc.
4501 Forbes Boulevard, Suite 200, Lanham, Maryland 20706
http://www.rowmanlittlefield.com

Estover Road, Plymouth PL6 7PY, United Kingdom

Copyright © 2011 by Tim R. McDonald

British Library Cataloguing in Publication Information Available

Library of Congress Cataloging-in-Publication Data

McDonald, Tim R., 1985–
  Unsustainable : a strategy for making public schooling more productive, effective, and affordable / Tim R. McDonald.
      p. cm. — (Innovations in education, no. 9)
  Includes bibliographical references.
  ISBN 978-1-60709-364-0 (cloth : alk. paper) — ISBN 978-1-60709-365-7 (pbk. : alk. paper) — ISBN 978-1-60709-366-4 (ebook)
   1. Public schools—United States. 2. School improvement programs—United States. 3. Education—Parent participation—United States. 4. Public schools—State supervision—United States. 5. Government aid to education—United States—States. I. Title.
  LA217.M274 2011
  371.2'07—dc22   2010034997

Printed in the United States of America

For my family

Student moves on.

Contents

Illustrations

FIGURES

TABLES

Foreword

Ted Kolderie

This important book comes at a critical time in our country's discussion about how to improve learning and its learning system.

We are at the end of a long period in which interest and concern has been rising . . . in which the focus of policymaking has moved beyond the local district up as far as the national government . . . in which the idea has been to specify what students should know and be able to do . . . and in which the conviction has grown that "accountability" is the driver for change.

Policymaking is deep into mandates and requirements, and into standards and standardization. There is a powerful desire to find "what works" and to specify the use of those practices.

Yet there is, as Tim McDonald shows here, a fundamental and growing problem with the financial sustainability of our public elementary/secondary system—for which greater productivity is the only real response.

And this requires us to appreciate that we are now at a turning point in the cycle of improvement. After these years of standardizing—working out variation—it is time now to reintroduce variation. Innovation is the essence of productivity: people trying and testing new approaches not currently in use.

This kind of thing, innovation, is enormously difficult for a system governed politically—and so, especially difficult for public education, dominated as it is by the notion of "real school."

As the author shows here, the only conceivable answer is the "split screen"—the idea, new to education policy, of states and districts running a set of innovative schools side-by-side with the traditional schools.

Only?

It is a feasible idea. The split screen—the choice for users and for employees between the comfortable traditional model and the new-but-yet-unproven model—is the process of change in almost all our systems. It has simply not been the process for education policy; caught up as policymaking has so long been in the search for the one best way.

This relates to another important, powerful idea in the book, which has to do with the country cutting a new deal with teachers.

- Most of those in the policy discussion now affirm the central importance of good teachers and good teaching in the effort to lift the levels of learning.
- In most of the systems in which change moves successfully, what drives it is the decisions of users about what improvements work best. Think about communications systems, transportation systems, computer systems.

We could think about teachers as "the users" in the learning system, knowing the differences in interest and in aptitude among their students, needing to select the learning methods and materials that will best help their students as individuals, or trying things not tried before—innovating as practitioners.

Readers will, I hope, come away from this book with a sense of the need and the potential for people in the policy world to find a way to meld successfully their now-divergent attitudes toward teachers and toward teacher unions.

Teachers currently are popular; teacher unions currently are not. The impulse at the moment is to treat the unions as the principal obstacle to reform.

That is unlikely to succeed. The attitudes and the behavior of the unions are a product of the way school is arranged: Today it is simply not a model in which the professionals are trusted to know how the job is best done. People who would never try to tell their electrician how to do his or her job think nothing of telling teachers how to do their job.

Through their unions, whose leadership they elect, teachers are saying essentially that they are unwilling to be held accountable for things they do not control. Few reasonable people would be. I wouldn't. You wouldn't.

There is a simple answer: Give teachers the real authority to arrange student learning, in return for which it will be reasonable to ask them to accept responsibility for student and school success. This is a deal the unions will have every reason to accept: They have long wanted to win a professional role as well as economic security for their members.

Again: The new arrangement will be best introduced gradually and voluntarily, using the split-screen strategy for change.

All this is laid out in this book. Its major contribution is a set of new and nontraditional policy ideas. They should get broad and serious attention.

This mis-understands (mis-represents) the complex role of unions + power.

It also doesn't recognize the role of poverty in education.

Preface

This book frames a problem and provides a strategy to address it. It strives to show something that many education professionals and policymakers have come to believe but rarely mention, declaring what has never been argued in public: that this country's current system of K–12 schooling is not financially viable and is becoming more inefficient year by year. ~really?

One effect of growing, emergency federal funding for K–12 education has been to create an impression that schools are suffering because of the economic downturn. This is true. But the downturn is not the sole reason for their financial pains . . . nor is it the principal reason.

As Education|Evolving partners and associates have worked around the country, it has become increasingly apparent that the annual routine of raising spending and cutting services to balance school budgets cannot continue. There is a collective acknowledgement by many school administrators that the system is not sustainable. They sense, as one superintendent has put it, that they are merely "managing decline."

For decades local, state, and federal governments have increased spending to match education expenditures that have regularly outpaced economic growth. Beginning in 2008 this was no longer possible, compelled by the economic contraction of the recession and now perpetuated by growing claims from other important public services, such as care for the aging and medical and hospital services.

It is difficult to imagine doing things differently in schooling, perhaps because we are so used to the factory model or perhaps because there is no one clear alternative. This is unimaginative. The future will require a new way of thinking: more decentralized, more professional roles for teachers, more innovation.

The future will also require new and fundamentally different models. The task of reform is not to find a magical new technology nor to find one new model that will be the future—but to put in place conditions that make it most likely technologies will be taken up and applied to improve learning and contain costs by remaking schooling.

At the system level, this will require continuing to open public schooling to innovators and establishing and safeguarding autonomy for schools that seek to be different. At the school level, this will require new forms of management that increasingly place teachers in positions of authority, empowering the "users" of public education to drive innovation.

The traditional batch processing, "factory" style of school is underproductive. The system that runs and oversees these schools is unlikely (or unable) to facilitate the type of innovation necessary to make significant gains in performance and productivity. For years we have been covering up this reality with added spending. Can the country afford this without better results?

This book is about improving the cost and effectiveness of public schooling through a strategy of innovation to improve productivity. It provides policy recommendations at the state, district, and federal levels. In a final chapter, it outlines uncommon strategies for overcoming some of the most difficult political, practical, and structural roadblocks to improvement.

The writing of this book coincided with the financial crisis of 2008–2010, which exacerbated but did not cause the existing structural problems. We are at the front end of a wave, one that we can respond to but cannot change. The task now is to take a static system rooted in uniformity and continue turning it toward one that is dynamic and self-improving, one that captures the collective expertise and energies of everyone in American society. The goal is a well-functioning education system that continually innovates to improve performance and cost. This is systemic change, and the main actors may well be those that are at present listened to least—teachers and students. Together with new technologies and new school designs, they may participate in the same kind of user-driven innovation that has transformed information industries from news media to higher education. It is happening already.

I am optimistic that the country will be able to figure this out.

Acknowledgments

The content of this book draws from the thinking and the experience of some of the best minds at work on the theory, strategy, and methods required to change large systems.

This work is taking place at the Center for Policy Studies, through its project Education|Evolving in partnership with Hamline University and many associates and colleagues in Minnesota and around the country.

Education|Evolving has learned a good deal from the work of Clayton Christensen of Harvard Business School on the character and change of large organizations. Our managing partner, Curt Johnson, co-wrote *Disrupting Class: How Disruptive Innovation Will Change the Way the World Learns* (2008) with Christensen and Michael Horn, applying their concept of disruptive innovation to the public school system of K–12.

Walt McClure chairs the Center for Policy Studies. A theoretical physicist by training, Walt has applied scientific thinking to the design and function of large social systems, effectively creating a new way of looking at the world—large-system architecture—that is as sound as it is uncommon.

Ted Kolderie has brought his own systemic perspective into education with Joe Graba and those involved with the E|E operation. This includes a remarkable and complementary team: John Boland, Ed Dirkswager, Kim Farris-Berg, Curt Johnson, Lars Johnson, Dan Loritz, John Parr, Jon Schroeder, Mark Van Ryzin, and Bob Wedl.

This combination has resulted in a capacity to move the needle on rethinking and re-forming schooling in an industry caricatured for its obstinacy.

For that we thank our funders, past, present, and future, who have understood—sometimes intuitively, sometimes by observing results—the significance of the systemic perspective in the quiet work the center does.

Particular acknowledgment and thanks go to Bob Brown and Tom Koerner; Jack Witkin and Verne Johnson; Tom Atkinson at the Information Technology and Innovation Foundation; Walter Enloe at Hamline University; and the Civic Caucus, the public affairs outfit where some of this book's core ideas were worked through.

On a personal level, I would like to thank my family and the leaders of the organizations named above, who have taken the time to invite a few younger people to work with them. They do not have to, and that they do is a testament to their character and humility. Dan Loritz, for one, has a way of recognizing potential and helping people and organizations progress. In his unassuming way, Dan is making a deep, meaningful imprint on society.

This book is an effort at rethinking assumptions about school design, regulation, and productivity. It seeks to move an important set of questions into the minds of those who are, or may become, involved with reshaping public schooling. Importantly, it attempts not just to describe the way things are—to "sit back and admire the problem," as Curt Johnson says—but also to provide viable policy proposals and strategy to bring them to fruition.

There are many good people at work on this, and through their endeavors the system might just be made to run a little better.

Introduction

A Toolbox of Ways to Rethink Schooling

This United States is entering a time of rethinking some basic assumptions about the design and function of its public school system. The process is being compelled by problems with performance, pressures from unsustainable costs, and the rise of alternative school models that have made it clear some kind of fundamental change is inevitable. It is already under way.

When doing this rethinking, it is necessary to divide the goals society has for public schooling from the particular system set up to pursue them. This can help policymakers determine how the goals have changed. In K–12 schools, for example, the goal for 100 years was to ensure access for students. Now the task is to have all students perform at high levels. Our system accomplished the first goal remarkably well, but it is not designed to accomplish the second.

The strategic options available to school leaders to balance the budget can be represented by a quadrant Ted Kolderie put together during the economic contraction of 2009. There are short-term and long-term solutions to balancing a budget, he figured. Over the short term, policymakers and administrators may tax to increase revenue and cut services to decrease expenditures. Over the long term, the state may work to increase revenue by working to help the private sector increase the economy.

"We are going to need to rethink how we do this," Dan Loritz said in 2010, casting a career of executive experience in schooling against the financing challenges of the past decade. "And [we will need to] redesign how we do this. Every state is the same. We've been doing it this way for so long that we can't think of any other way to do it. But we're

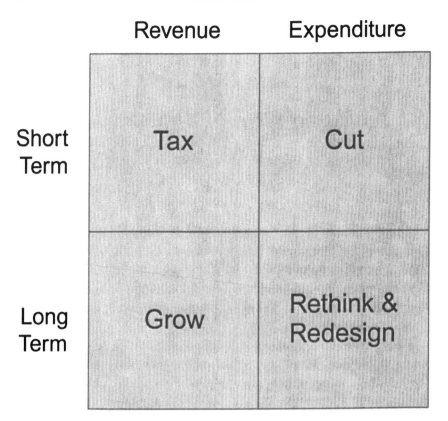

Figure I.1.   Rethinking growth

going to have to find a way to do it with high quality, good outcomes, with less resources."[1]

To help in the process of rethinking school and regulatory design, Ted Kolderie assembled a list of different methods for re-forming how things are done:

Termination—cutting out a service.

Prevention—avoiding or delaying the onset of high-cost services.

Substitution—changing the way things are done, such as supported self-help.

Competition—opening a service to more than one supplier or manager.

Utilization—getting more or better service from existing personnel, equipment, or infrastructure.

Capitation—give teachers and school leaders the money and let them keep for the school what they do not spend.

Regulation—requiring actions or functions.

Deregulation—opening up the system; creating incentives to do things differently.

Throughout this book, at the end of every chapter, there are suggestions for improving the cost and productivity of K–12. Each idea follows one of these tools for redesign, as a sort of demonstration exercise. They represent just a few of the ways that the functions of schooling can be rethought. In the processes of innovating, these methods may be employed regularly by practitioners, managers, and regulators alike.

Part One

A STRATEGY FOR IMPROVEMENT

Change is happening very quickly now, both in the pace of the world and in the progress of technology. The question facing policymakers and education leaders is not one of seeing what is to come, but of creating the conditions to be continually innovating to find new and better ways of doing things. The choice is between managing decline or managing change. K–12 must be made into a self-improving system.

Placing two bets for improvement.

To do this EducationlEvolving advocates that policymakers run a split-screen effort at operating schools, continuing to improve traditional schools while creating a separate, independent sector where the work of innovation may take place—including its own regulatory structure, tuned particularly to the needs of an innovation sector.

Innovation is necessary in a changing world. Best practice is never static. Technology is always progressing. The conditions of society evolve, and the context of the world changes. The demands on the system are intensifying, and the assignment put to it today is different than in the past. We are asking schools to perform at levels they were not designed to perform at. *But, fundamentally, people changes lowly.*

Innovation is something that happens when the fundamentals of a system are set right. In a well-functioning education system, productivity, effectiveness, and cost are improved upon as a function of its operation. Entrepreneurs and professionals are allowed to contribute, and incentives encourage pursuit of self-interest in service of the public interest.

A large system needs a place where the work of innovation may occur. Combining innovations in technology with innovations in the business model of school is radical work. In a system rooted in orthodoxy, it is iconoclastic.

This strategy hedges the nation's bets against any one single effort at improvement, either going all-out on trying to improve existing schools and the factory model, or trying all-new things all the time. It is also more politically viable. No one should be compelled to attend or work in the innovative schools. This is a matter of choice. Reciprocally, the innovative sector must be on equal footing with traditional schools. No protectionism—demand should be allowed to drive the scope and scale of innovation.

Chapter One

Redesigning the System

No system is permanent or can remain static while the world around it changes. Technology evolves, market demands alter, new competitors arise, new needs must be met. America's public schooling enterprise has the privilege of being able to observe and learn from other industries that have managed these conditions successfully, and from those that succumbed to them.

Newspapers have given way to blogs and online news sources. Professionally produced encyclopedias have been upstaged by the user-generated content of Wikipedia. Blockbuster found that it could not compete with the convenience of Netflix. The establishment of the music industry, with record labels and agents controlling the development of talent, is being disrupted by online user-controlled networks. Music stores are becoming obsolete, as iTunes has cornered the paid-for dissemination of music over the Web. Travel agencies, financial services, and other intermediary services are no longer needed in the same numbers as before—the effects of the long march toward disintermediation.

Naomi Stanford has put together a chart of traditional and new business models as part of a book on organizational design. (See table 1.1.)[2]

In each of these cases, the business model paradigm of the industry changed right from under the feet of otherwise strong, established, and competently managed organizations. The change in business model was enabled by new technologies. While the change was destabilizing for a time, each industry was ultimately improved and the customers benefited most. The same will occur for education. We have got the information technologies, but the business models—design of schools, format of learning, cost structure—are yet to catch up. When they do, the shift will be quick and dramatic.

Table 1.1. **Traditional versus New Business Models**

Traditional Model	New Model
Press release	RSS feed
Marketing collateral	Blog
Media tour	Webcast
Event	Social network
Customer reference	Community advocate
Data sheets	E-newsletters
Newspapers	Blogs
E-mail newsletters	Syndication (RSS)
Encyclopedia	Wikipedia
Phone	Skype, IM
Classifieds	Craigslist
Music stores	iTunes
Blockbuster	Netflix
Traditional music industry	MySpace, podcasts
TV	Rich web media, video blogs
Radio	Podcasts, XM radio
Travel agencies	Online travel websites
Magazines	Blogs, RSS
Talent agents (music, film)	MySpace, blogs, social networking
Middleperson	Internet
Banks/financial services	Online banking

The first priority of lawmakers should be to set up an education system that is capable of changing with the times.

There is no way to anticipate all the economic, technological, and cultural changes that will sweep the world in the years to come. Schools must be designed and the system must be arranged so that public education can respond and does not again get mired in a static state.

Cost and effectiveness are a top priority, Dexter Fletcher of the Institute for Defense Analyses has said, but the question for the defense industry is how to prepare for the unexpected. Structuring yourself so that you can respond to the unexpected is their business in the defense industry. They cannot plan out a strategy step by step, comprehensively, at the beginning and hold to it. Conditions are always changing.

So there is a need to separate the church from the faith, as Dan Loritz puts it. There are particular desirables in an education process: personalized experience, tutoring, the ability to pursue one's own interests under the hand of some guidance. These are aspects that can be achieved in any number of settings, from physical classrooms to virtual and blended online/in-person settings. Policymakers and education leaders must work to carve out the task of learning form the man-made organizations responsible for carrying it out.

If this core question is separated from the existing forms of schools, it quickly becomes apparent that it is possible to create effective schools in any number of forms.

INTERDEPENDENT SYSTEMS
RESIST COMPREHENSIVE CHANGE

At the system level, factory schools are a function of the legal and regulatory apparatus of states, with influence from Washington, and administered locally. At the school level course schedules, term calendars, and even the physical layout of schools contribute to its monolithic and rigid character. The relationship between the schools and the system is mutually reinforcing. Factory schools must form to agency policy, and the agencies exist to regulate factory schools.

Schools are driven toward standardization by this interdependence. Change is difficult because if one part changes they all must change. Lengthening the school day affects busing and sports. Introducing technology-mediated learning runs into prohibitive problems of classroom space, curriculum design, and scheduling.

Customization within the system is exceedingly expensive because it involves taking the existing structure and buying-down class size by hiring more teachers, building more classrooms, and expanding support services.

Instead, design schools in a modular structure. While customization is prohibitively costly in an interdependent system—it is three times more expensive to teach a student on an Individual Learning Plan (ILP)—it is necessary to break apart from uniform education to improve performance. An alternative approach is to reorganize the system and schools into a decentralized structure with an appropriate regulatory scheme, so that one component of the system can change without necessarily affecting the others. A modular architecture allows for customization.

INTRODUCE VARIABILITY INTO THE SYSTEM

From his position as editor of *The Economist* newspaper in 19th-century England, Walter Bagehot reflected on the innovative and progressive characteristics of the United States and Britain—their ability to adapt quickly and to always be improving as societies. He found their capacity for progress to be attributable to "variability" and to the interplay among people and industries that lead to competition and improvement. Variability precedes progress. In 1873 he wrote,

> Men progress, when they have a certain sufficient amount of variability in their nature. . . . The beginning is marked by an intense legality; that legality is the very condition of its existence, the bond which ties it together; but that legality—that tendency to impose a settled customary yoke upon all men and all action . . . kills out the variability implanted by nature. Progress is only possible in those happy cases where the force of legality has gone far enough to bind the nation together, but not far enough to kill out all varieties and destroy [the] perpetual tendency to change.[3]

So in the early stages of a system, Bagehot argued, stiff laws, customs, and uniformity are appropriate (even required) for the establishment of basic cultures and processes. This is true for school—the factory model was necessary and appropriate for expanding mandatory publicly funded education throughout the country. But at some point the uniformity changes from enabling to restricting, and degrees of variability must be allowed for so that improvement can occur.

Variability has been achieved steadily over the past two decades, state by state, in the forms of in-district and inter-district choice of school, state chartering of schools, and the creation of innovation zones inside school districts. These changes in the system are structural and provide platforms upon which innovations in schools and learning models may occur.

School governance must also change to enable variability and innovation in teaching and learning. While centralized control may be necessary in the beginning, Bagehot argued that total control of a system "tends to keep men fixed." The very characteristics that made it useful in the establishment of the system make it unfit for later stages in its evolution. "It prevents men from passing into the first age of progress—the very slow and very gradually improving age."

Deregulate to open up and get people thinking about innovation, Bagehot said. The factory school is not a place where improvement will occur because it is not a place where fundamental innovation may effectively take place. "Deliverance from the yoke of custom and uniformity develops an inquisitive and inventive mind."

COMBINE NEW TECHNOLOGIES
WITH NEW BUSINESS MODELS

Combining new technologies with new models enables jumps in performance and efficiency. The early age of modern American education was the standardized age—the time for establishing the system, which was no small task for such a large and diverse a country. The past century shows a tendency toward growth, expanding access into rural areas, up through age 18, involving all genders, races, and social and economic classes. The progress was quick at first. It was blunt and crude. Expansion was the game, and it moved as fast as it could.

Eventually progress slowed, then stopped. Fine-tuning began. The system improved. It ran better, more efficiently, more effectively. The gains were quick at first, as teaching methods were explored, training programs established, and best practices found.

This worked, and education progressed. But then changes stopped having large effects. The point of diminishing returns was reached. When it came time to shift from the old age of standardization to the new age of variation and customization, the improvement of the school was limited by the fixed model. And the capacity of the teacher was limited by the fixed design of the school. A larger perspective is now required. A jump has to be made.

Jumps are enabled by the advent of new technologies and their pairing with innovations in business models. Using new technologies to remake the learning process opens the door to a new plane of improvement. It takes progress made in effective teaching and learning styles, and it leverages them.

This country is in an awkward middle period now, hesitant to move. Progress began to slow once before, and we were jostled into action by the launch of Sputnik. It slowed again, and we are now stuck. We have yet to make the jump into the new age.

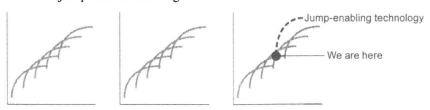

Figure 1.1. Enabling jumps in school performance

FACILITATE AND APPLY DISRUPTIVE TECHNOLOGIES

Disruptive technologies are those that enable an operation to serve the needs and interests of its customers in a fundamentally new and better way. These may be found by combining innovations in technology with innovations in the business model of schools.

Established players try at first to respond to a disruptive innovation by doing what they are already doing, only better. Much as the airlines disrupted railroads, computers replaced typewriters, and discount retailing surpassed the department store, so will new technologies of schooling blow away the factory model in their ability to personalize learning and improve productivity. Christensen writes that "disruption solves the more fundamental question: How do we make education more affordable?" Disruption is an "appropriate and necessary step" in making K–12 education more appropriate and effective in the information age.[4]

It is very difficult for a system of large, uniform, and centrally managed schools to operate an effective development program of small, decentralized, and flexible school designs. These are two different business models, requiring their own cultural and regulatory context. To be successful in the latter, a second operation needs to be set up around the new venture.

Ted Kolderie describes how this strategy was followed by Dayton-Hudson Corporation when the board of directors started Target in the 1960s. They understood that the retail upstart would invariably compete on some levels with department stores, and incentives would be strong for management to try to snuff the stores out.

But for the health of the entire company, Target needed the room and ability to mature. If retailing was going to be the future, existing interests could not thwart it. This was a two-bet strategy by Dayton-Hudson: Continue to improve the existing department stores, while running a full-fledged effort at cultivating and developing an entirely new design.

In public education there are the factory-model schools, which have been the norm and will continue to be preferred by many students. But there is also demand for schools that are fundamentally different. When the upstarts are put under the authority of the established, an artificial ceiling is built in. The more successful alternatives become, the more appeal they have and the more students will choose them over existing traditionally arranged schools. The political and financial pressures are strong for district management to keep these options under their thumb and prevent their proliferation.

One teacher-leader from a major urban area said during a meeting about teacher-run schools—one form of redesign—in her district, "We could become as successful as we wanted, but could not expand beyond one building. As long as we stayed a novelty, we were all right because we didn't seriously affect their enrollment."

When the world changes, when technologies evolve, it is the upstarts that have the edge. Established organizations are often set up to self-perpetuate. How they allocate resources, their culture, and their governance all work on improving what is already there.

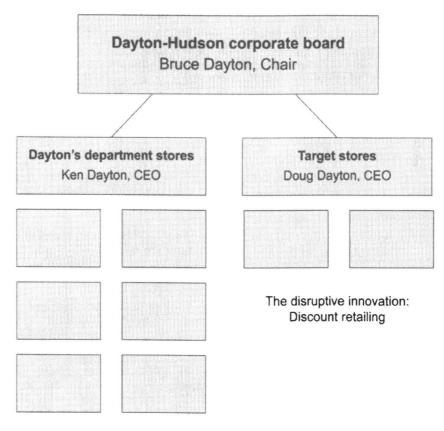

Figure 1.2. **The Target model of managing change**

The 'Target Model' for Managing Disruptive Innovation.

How Dayton-Hudson became the only department store in America to successfully transition to discount retailing.

Autonomy for start-ups, for innovations, is important. Essential.

Harvard Business School professor Clayton Christensen argues an approach to innovation that is as prescient for education as it is for industry. To facilitate serious change, he has found, large and complex organizations may find it best to create a new organizational space that is both within the company, yet independent from existing cultures and processes.

The idea is that there are times when the foundations of an industry shift, usually due to the introduction of new technologies. Buggies did not become automobiles, they were replaced by automobiles. The railroads did not transform into airlines, they were usurped by them. Typewriters did not evolve into computers, they were overtaken by them.

It can be exceptionally difficult for the managers of one technology to continue to serve their present customers while also innovating to get out ahead of future interests—a customer base that may not yet exist. The pressure is to spend limited resources on current demand.

"When disruptive change appears, managers...actually need to run two businesses in tandem, one whose processes are tuned to the existing business model and another that is geared toward the new model."

Here is an example from retailing, and the experience of Minnesota's Target Corp:

The five Dayton brothers had taken over the family's large and successful, high-class department store in downtown Minneapolis in the 1950's. They saw the region growing beyond the old city. They responded by opening department stores in the suburbs. Then at a convention about 1958 they heard a discussion about 'discounting.'

Talking about this afterward they found discounting unattractive in some respects. But attractive as well. In 1960 they went into discounting—by creating a wholly-owned subsidiary, Target Stores. Douglas Dayton became its CEO. Two stores opened in 1962. They were immediately successful.

Quickly the department store group was complaining about Target cutting into its business. "But I didn't report to Ken" (his brother, who headed Dayton's Department Stores), Doug Dayton says. "I reported to Bruce as chair of the corporate board." Of all the department store groups in America—some 300—only Dayton-Hudson made the transition successfully into discount retailing. Today the whole corporation bears the name Target.

The same holds for education. Much as the upstart Target Stores were able to grow and expand free from resistance from the department store executives *(You're stealing our business!)*, innovative public schools will need to have their own protected space where they can develop independent of interests that may not have incentive to see them succeed. **Under this model, innovation zones should report to the district board of education, not the central administration—which, structurally, is more akin to the department stores. It is the district board that is charged with overseeing all options, providing the best schools possible, without favor for any particular organizational space.**

Note: Excerpted from Kolderie, *Creating the Capacity for Change* (2004)

Figure 1.2. (*continued*)

As options for schools emerge outside of the factory model, there will be excess capacity in districts. This can be disconcerting. As enrollment declines so does revenue, and the price per head of the factory school rises. The district becomes increasingly top heavy, allocating a larger and larger share of pupil funding to overhead. As the district contracts, a larger portion of remaining students will be those who are the most challenging to serve.

In private industry this creation of excess capacity results in restructuring, merger, or, if a company does not respond, bankruptcy. It will do no good to continue to subsidize the status quo for schools. It is only staving off the inevitable reorganization or dissolution.

The task of education leaders and those designing public policy is to facilitate the process of disruption so that it minimizes the negative side effects and maximizes the public good. Disruptions are threats only in so far as one refuses to imagine the alternatives. Really, they are remarkable growth opportunities. It is during times of disruption that the needle really moves.

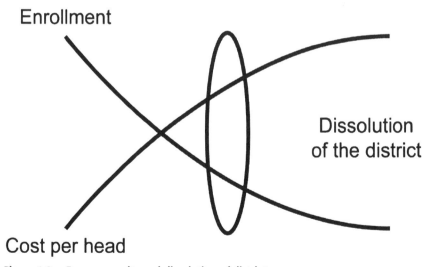

Figure 1.3.   Excess capacity and dissolution of districts

CREATE AN INDEPENDENT UNIT
WHERE INNOVATION MAY OCCUR

Serious research and development (R & D) requires space for innovation, with characteristics adept to the processes of exploring, cultivating, and developing ideas.

The separate space must be protected. "We were fine," one teacher remarked in a discussion about teacher-run schools with policymakers, "until we demonstrated success and wanted to replicate." The existing structure and professional interests did not know how to handle them. Pressures came to bear from all sides—administration, unions, families— not to change things. They crowded out the voices of students and teachers who want and need something different.

In an autonomous setting, a team devoted to an innovation can work with a smaller group of students. Smaller schools with staff dedicated to the work can create an appropriate and constructive attitude for the setbacks that occur in any new effort. They will be energized by small wins and are better positioned to recognize and build on progress.

An innovative culture requires a different process of resource allocation, different ways of making decisions, and different mechanisms for measuring success. Creating an independent organization with architecture that encourages and supports innovation does not guarantee success—but it does make it possible. It provides a space for teams to work toward innovation, instead of fighting inertia.

We should not expect existing schools to innovate with fundamentally new organizational models. Predictably, they have resisted (think of the antipathy to the chartering process). Serious school model innovations will be performed by new entrants. Lawmakers should be wary of calls from those with vested interests in the existing system to artificially limit or shut down the newcomers. Regulation should facilitate evolution toward improvement, not outlaw it.

Instead of attempting to remake the entire system in one fell swoop, policy should stage changes, simply opening up to entrepreneurs and those with ideas for improvement. Demand will drive supply if we let it. Release people from the yoke of custom and uniformity, and they will begin to stretch their creative minds. This is healthiest, most politically feasible, and most responsive to needs in the system.

It also helps capture the collective expertise and efforts of people beyond the management and planners. People do know how to meet student needs. Throughout the country, entrepreneurs are figuring out how to get high results from students who otherwise are not doing well in traditional factory schools. Often these leaders are teachers, education leaders, and sometimes noneducators with particular interests and skills—especially in IT.— *Hardly.*

The question for policy is how to capture and direct the collective knowledge and expertise of all these individuals. The process starts by creating a place where people can continually work on ways to better teach and learn, incorporate new technology, and improve productivity.

MOVE TOWARD A "SUPER MODEL" OF SCHOOL

An independent school using technology-mediated learning constitutes a "super model" that can move on multiple fronts at once. It can facilitate mass customization, change form, and innovate to work on cost and effectiveness in real time, every day.

The super model can be teacher-led or principal-led. The technology-mediated learning may be through project-based learning, intelligent tutoring, or other processes that differentiate the pace and content of learning. While the super model can take many forms, it has consistent characteristics:

- It is lightly regulated and held accountable to a performance contract with some government authority.
- The teachers are wholly or at least partially responsible for the budget and may keep for the school what they do not spend.
- Administrative functions of the school are often separated from, and made submissive to, the professional teaching functions.
- The schools are much smaller and make creative use of contracting to meet any service needs—including advanced and specialty courses.
- Students do a larger part of the laboring, through technology-mediated learning. *And what will motivate them to do so?*
- They combine innovations in technology with innovations in organizational and business models to achieve a new form.

This model moves school from teaching-centered to learning-centered, removing the structural limitation on productivity that has held back factory schools for years.

Autonomy enables, and discretion over spending encourages, school leaders to innovate to drive down costs. The schools that follow this super-model arrangement regularly run at a fraction of the cost of neighboring factory schools, and sometimes at half the per-pupil cost of the most inefficient districts (see Minneapolis in figure 1.4).

The schools are innovations in themselves, by virtue of being different from the factory model. But their greater contribution is as a platform for innovation and as the engines of innovation, where the act of innovating is played out by teachers and students every day.

The productivity of the traditional model is capped at the physical capacity of the teacher. Its variable is class size. In the super model, differentiated pace and content make it possible to apply learning models in which students take direction of their work and provide the labor in a process of supported self-help. Intelligent tutoring, learning management systems, and the Internet are tools—innovations in technology. They must be paired with innovations in school models to make full use of them.

Any marginal increase in effort by students will be significant. And for those presently checked out, any increase will be immediately felt. If there are 25 students in a classroom with one teacher and the students give

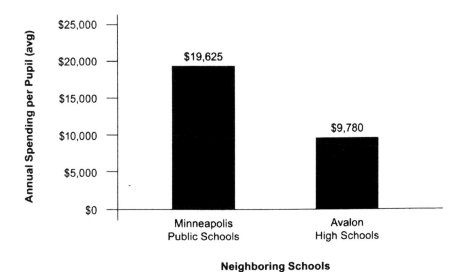

Figure 1.4.   Cost discrepancy of factory versus super models of schools

The **super model of school** is an organizational arrangement that opens a school up to continual innovation and self-improvement. Leaders at the school save money by being creative and resourceful, and making liberal use of contracting to cover service needs. In order to do this the school is small, autonomous, and lightly regulated—held accountable for results.

Figure 1.5. The super model of school

an average of 50 percent more effort—entirely possible in a technology-mediated environment—the net labor in the classroom would increase approximately 12 times.

Perhaps most importantly, this model moves away from the teacher-lecture model that caps school productivity at the physical capacity of the paid professional. By enlisting student labor and using technology to differentiate the pace of learning, these schools make it possible to achieve an entirely new level of productivity.

As resources decline in real terms, the only way schools can maintain quality—and to improve it—is to find improvements in productivity.

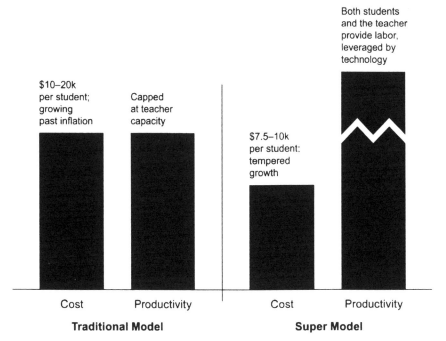

Figure 1.6. The economics of the super model of school

This model is a paradigm shift. For policy, regulation, and research stuck in the old paradigm, this super model makes no sense—and so it is overlooked. But these schools are going to proliferate in the coming decade, as more schools are created in the "open sectors" of autonomous district innovation zones (such as Boston's pilot schools) and chartering. They offer a place where the problems of cost, productivity, and effectiveness can be worked on in real time by those on the front lines. It is a self-diagnosing and self-improving model of school.

Capitation

Let Schools Control Their Budget and Keep What They Do Not Spend

Give schools a lump sum. Let them make spending decisions and keep what is left over. When schools pay for services and may keep for school activities what they do not spend, expenditures go down. Establish deliverables and grant teachers the authority to do things as they see fit. Tell them what to do but not how to do it, and judge on results. Not only does this give teachers ownership, but it leads to more efficient and effective spending. It is a driver for innovation.

What are these in learning?
How do we measure?
Age-old problem.

Chapter Two

Change Requires a Viable Strategy

In large and complex systems, the entrenchment of interests is inherent, and a challenge. But it is not true that serious education reform is destined to failure because of it. Good ideas alone do not move. Interests do not converge and problems do not get solved just because they should. Goals require strategies. Hope, conviction, and good intentions—important as they are—are not strategies for improvement or change.

Every goal requires a strategy, and strategies need methods. Public education exists in a dynamic political environment, with legislative processes fortified against rapid and comprehensive change. To improve the performance of the education system, policy must impact the behavior of students, teachers, and administrators. The way to affect behavior is to identify and target what it is that causes people to act as they do. This requires the discernment of incentives, positive or negative, and tracing them up the frame of the system to find their origin.

Students play games on their cell phones in study hall instead of working. Why? Because they are not motivated to do class work. Why are they not motivated? Because school is boring. Why is school boring? Could be a few reasons: The content of class is too easy, too hard, or seems irrelevant; the class is too slow; the way school is set up does not make sense to them.

Some people may think: *Tough if they don't like it. Who does?* Yet if achievement matters, then performance matters. If performance matters, then effort matters. And if effort matters, then motivation is central. If students playing games in study hall are a metaphor for their entire approach to school, then we do in fact have quite a problem.

Dropping out, checking out, and underachieving are ubiquitous and chronic—not a peculiarity to only a few students. At some point, blame for the widespread failure falls to the system. When a military campaign fails, it is the general who is accountable. Not the officers, and not the soldiers. When policy fails—and when it fails uniformly across the country—the fault lies in its framing, not those tasked with carrying it out.

State laws form school systems, which create the districts and schools. The behaviors we see in the classroom have their origin in regulation and law. Legislation directs rule making, from which the character of schools and the dynamics and incentives around them get their form. Reorganizing out in the field, or pumping in more supplies, will not make up for a faulty policy designed up on the hill.

THE LIMITATIONS OF K–12 REFORM EFFORTS TO DATE

States have been focusing on improving K–12 education in the United States for more than two decades, but they have been doing so on the assumption that the problem to be addressed is a performance problem that can be solved by pushing the existing educational model to do better. In recent years, two approaches to educational reform—standards-based reform and chartering schools—have in different ways been trying to generate better schools.

Lately the principal means for trying to improve educational performance has been standards-based reform. Initially designed in 1990, standards-based reform was based on the idea that school districts would respond to the call to improve as "objective" standards highlighted progress or lack thereof. When states did not improve or did not improve as much as was expected, policymakers became impatient and moved to "require" improvement, through steps such as the No Child Left Behind Act.

Another major educational reform effort in the United States has been the school chartering movement, which emerged first in Minnesota in 1991 and has since spread in one form or another to 40 states, plus the District of Columbia.

Unlike the standards movement, the chartering movement was an institutional innovation that broke open the exclusive that districts had in the creation and management of schools. It was the first major foray to introduce variability into public education—for "creating the capacity for change," as the book by Ted Kolderie is titled.

As originally conceived, chartered schools could be created and run by—even authorized by—entities other than local boards of education. Laws enabling chartering made different models possible by opening the way for less regulated and more autonomous schools. However, these laws did not themselves innovate with forms of schooling.

Chartering is a platform on which schools of various kinds can be built. A chartered school is not a kind of school in any pedagogical sense—the common term "charter school" is misleading. Unfortunately, too many chartered schools have simply replicated the pedagogy of traditional schools, with the predictable lack of improvement.

Some progress has been made through standards-based reform and chartering schools. Standards, supplemented by assessment and the introduction of consequences for nonperformance, have begun to move up the proportion of students proficient with basic skills. Chartering has proved unexpectedly popular and now represents more than 15 percent of public enrollment in a number of larger cities.   *Really?*

Yet everyone remains disappointed in the pace of progress and believes that more is needed and possible. The disappointment comes in part because the trend lines for educational improvement are so flat. High schools are unable to retain one in three students to graduation. And nearly half of the high school dropouts point to boredom and lack of interest in classes as a reason for leaving school.

Moreover, the students who do graduate from high school in the United States are not well prepared. In one survey, firms reported that 60 percent of applicants with a high school degree or GED were poorly prepared for an entry-level job. Respondents to a Conference Board survey rated high school graduates as deficient in 10 skills—including written communications, critical thinking, and teamwork—and excellent in no skills. Only about half of high school graduates have the reading skills they need to succeed in college, a rate that has not changed in 10 years.[5]

The disappointment in the pace of educational reform also comes from a sense that in our changing world the improvement is outpaced by the need for improvement. High school especially remains a major puzzle, with proficiency low, with gains in the elementary years falling off in the upper grades, and with large differences still in knowledge, skills, and graduation rates between racial groups.

To some, the situation with respect to U.S. education represents a failure of will. The country is not serious about improvement, they say.

If it were it would make educational standards even higher and courses even harder—as if tightening the status quo were the logical response to obsolescence. If the country were serious it would increase financing for K–12 education and pay teachers more. But funding alone cannot be the fundamental problem.

Concerns over funding, while legitimate, are a diversion from the real and more difficult challenges of system reform in public education. Many of the efforts at K–12 educational "reform" have been less about reform than about getting traditional schools to perform better—usually by making them do what they are doing now, only harder, longer, and with more added on. More tests. More homework. More math. Less recess. Fewer art and music classes. A longer school day. A longer school year.

Ever since the publication in 1983 of *A Nation at Risk*, the United States has been pressing its schools to do better. Standards and assessment and accountability have been introduced, professional training has been stepped up, and financing has been increased. The "improvement industry" at work on this job is enormous—countless individuals and organizations researching and publishing, speaking, writing and consulting; conducting professional development seminars; and advising and exhorting districts and schools to be better. With all this effort, over so long a period of time, why has there not been more success in improving schools and learning?

There is a culture around education that is long on pontification—especially in Washington, DC—but short on serious strategies. Without good strategies for improving the design of the system, people have shrunk back into ideological and professional camps.

It is time to consider that the cause of the failure to improve learning might lie precisely in this assumption that the problem is one of performance, to be solved by pushing the existing model to do better. This is not a strategy for achieving different results.

COMPREHENSIVE ACTION VERSUS TARGETED CHANGE

The essence of strategy is to position oneself to have options and room to maneuver. It is not to map out an entire campaign ahead of time, or as Robert Greene says, to carry out a brilliant plan that proceeds in steps.[6]

Comprehensive plans have practical limitations. They almost never get implemented from beginning to end. Leadership changes, conditions evolve, resources shift. It is impossible to predict precisely how students and teachers will respond to changes. When innovating, schools and districts need to be flexible. Comprehensive reform puts all the eggs in one basket. Who is going to hold the peddlers of these ideas to account? How would they be held to account? They will not be. We should be wary of that.

Some reformers clamor for large-scale frontal assaults, in an attempt to remake the system to some ideal form, all at once. Frontal attacks are compromised in the legislative process. They stiffen the resistance of those invested in the status quo, and they put the reformers at risk of seeming too radical and thus too risky.

Instead, strategy should seek to open the system little by little, allowing for change, and then work to get a process of innovation put in place. The dissatisfaction and latent unrest among teachers and students might turn into an active demand for change.

The strategy that Education|Evolving advocates, which Minnesota has exercised in a first-of-its-kind education reform, is to start something in that state, show it can work, then move it around the country. Bagehot observed that men are guided by type, not by argument. "Some winning instance must be set up before them," he said, "or the sermon will be in vain, and the doctrine will not spread."[7]

Exhortation is not a strategy. On the political side, people seem content to wage the futile frontal wars between, say, unions and advocates of vouchers, or otherwise push an agenda of reform that does not have much structural impact—more funding, or performance pay for teachers. The standards movement is rooted in demanding people do better.

These proposals, as John Brandl and Vin Weber wrote in a commission report to the Minnesota legislature in the 1990s, "all come down to exhorting people in government to do things differently. Exhortation is not a policy. It is not systematic. It is ignored with impunity. Urging people in government to manage better will not work without also changing the system in which they operate."[8]

PEOPLE PURSUE THEIR
SELF-INTEREST—AND THAT'S OKAY

Unless invested parties are able to act in some pursuit of their own self-interest, it is reasonable to expect reforms will encounter intractable resistance. It will not work to take the system head-on, with its established processes, interests, and administrators. Head-on attacks in large and complex systems almost never work.

A French diplomat was able to unite Europe after centuries of warring because he got people to acquiesce to the idea of a single economic union by pursuing their own interest. He anticipated, correctly, that once coal and steel were linked, not only would peace be designed into the continent (through shared control of "the tools and machinery of war") but that political and cultural union would follow.

He knew that the only way to get so many diverse actors moving in the right direction was to get incentives to be the driver. Arrange it so that the parties pursue the goal, by pursuing their self-interest.

There are other examples of this. When the district's site-governed schools law was being deliberated in Minnesota in 2009, teachers were the ones principally moving it through the legislature. They saw, as teacher unions are seeing now across the country, that the creation of new schools is an opportunity for teachers to gain a stake in reforms and improve the professional character of their job.

Superintendents supported the law because it expanded their capacity to respond to the independent and competitive nature of chartered schools. Legislators liked it because it further expanded choice, localized control, and continued to open the K–12 systems to change.

In a conference committee meeting one early spring evening, a conservative Republican leaned back in his chair and smiled. "Fewer mandates, more authority for teachers, greater local control . . . there is peace in the valley."

A Democrat followed: "The reason why this law (which effectively created in-district versions of chartered schools) is sailing through so quietly . . . is because of its common support" from unions, school districts, and business.[9]

RUN A SPLIT-SCREEN EFFORT

Policymakers should seek to create two separate operations in the public school system: the traditional and the innovative. While continuing to improve existing schools, there will need to be a separate place designed particularly for exploring fundamentally new and better ways of accomplishing learning. These are two different kinds of efforts, and they require sectors with special characteristics.

The strategy of the split screen that Ted Kolderie has put forth, which has guided many of the structural reforms of the past 20 years, has at its root the belief that public schooling cannot be remade to perfection in one fell swoop.

Large systems need a place where new ideas can be worked on, in the interest of improving and adapting to the future. People have varied needs, interests, and aptitudes, so many different kinds of schools need to be available.

There is a practical reason, too. Change is much easier when it is voluntary. Nobody should be compelled to attend or work in the innovative schools. Demand should be the driver for what innovations are provided.

The first phase of the split-screen strategy was to make change possible. The work in this sense is well underway. Most states have strong chartering laws, and the trends of cities and states is toward creating the capacity for doing things differently.

The time is right for a new phase in the split-screen strategy, developing the separate regulatory structures that are designed and tuned particularly to the needs of each sector. This will help clear up the work that is needed now among schools.

Innovation is necessary in a changing world. Best practice is never static. Technology is always progressing. The conditions of society evolve, and the context of the world changes. The demands on the system are intensifying and the assignment put to it today is different than in the past. We are asking schools to perform at levels they were not designed to perform at.

The innovative sectors in public education will rely on the government less for control and more for coordination. There is a larger role for associative bodies and consultancy services in the design and operation of schools—particularly with the use of IT. The people involved in the innovative sector need to be able to recognize the value of small victories and not be discouraged at the inevitable setbacks.

This strategy hedges the nation's bets against any one single effort at improvement. Nobody knows ahead of time what innovations will work out, because innovation is a process. In a situation where the future is uncertain, you create space to maneuver.

CREATE A SOUND SYSTEM FOR PUBLIC EDUCATION

The goal of policymakers should be to create a sound and active market in public schooling that allows for dynamism, competition, and quality control without hampering R & D.

Public schools have evolved now from a closed system to an open one. Since Minnesota began the choice movement in the 1980s with a series of systemic reforms, districts and states have been undergoing changes that further open the opportunity to create new schools and unbundle a system that was and still is highly interdependent.

Trends are away from professional government administrators and toward private nongovernmental management companies and entrepreneurs. States are moving away from a one-way teacher-certification process and toward alternatives that get more variety into the teaching force. Schools and districts are shedding their insularity and increasing partnerships for services with for-profit companies in IT and other industries.

Popular belief tends to assume that government schools cannot be run like the private market. It is of less importance, however, who the buyer of the schooling is than how the market is constructed. It is just as possible to have a poorly functioning private market as it is to have an optimal market funded and regulated by the government.

In order for a government education system to achieve the core characteristics of a dynamic market, teachers and students need to have the choice both of which school they choose to spend their time at, and what type of school. There has to be plurality among the schools. New entrants must be allowed to come in, as entrepreneurs and as teachers.

Since school is a significant public good, there will be processes to filter those schools less likely to succeed. But there must be set rules, fair play, and absolutely no protectionism.

The open sector is important in part because it can support successful schools and close failing ones. Failing schools that were created by charter are likely to close, which is precisely what ought to happen. Successful chartered schools are able to grow, which is also what should happen.

Too often, failing district schools are not put out of business and go on failing students for years—which should never be allowed to happen. And other successful district schools are not permitted to grow and take over from failing district schools.

CREATE A PLACE FOR R & D WORK TO OCCUR

A large system needs a place where the work of innovation may occur. Combining innovations in technology with innovations in the business model of school is radical work. In a system rooted in orthodoxy, it is iconoclastic. People will try to starve it, bleed it, and kill it.

Those companies that have achieved unusual longevity in their field, weathering changes of technology and society, did so by creating a space where bright people can get out ahead of changes.

Christensen describes how IBM was the only successful maker of mainframe computers to successfully transition into personal computing, in large part because it set up the PC operation as its own independent business unit. Their high-volume, low-margin personal computers were very different than the low-volume, high-margin super computers that customers were buying at the time.

Apple Inc. has survived as a small company against Microsoft by better identifying user needs and meeting them through "imagination without limits."[10] Their R & D operation runs a split-screen strategy on multiple fronts, pitting development units against one another in competition.

Similar to IBM's transition from mainframe to personal computing, Dayton-Hudson became the only department store chain to successfully transition into discount retailing—also by running a split-screen, creating a separate business unit called Target that was allowed to grow and develop insulated from the protest from the established sections of the corporation.

Each of these companies started the new things small. They funded them, encouraged them, and protected them. The innovation sector of a split screen should be allowed to grow in response to demand. This is appropriate and necessary, for the good of the entire enterprise.

Innovation is something that happens when the fundamentals of a system are set right. In a well-functioning education system, productivity, effectiveness, and cost are improved upon as a function of its operation. Entrepreneurs and professionals are allowed to contribute, and incentives encourage pursuit of self-interest in service of the public interest.

Certain organizational models are more likely to lead to innovation than others. Figure 2.1 charts the likelihood that various arrangements will result in a rethinking of learning processes.

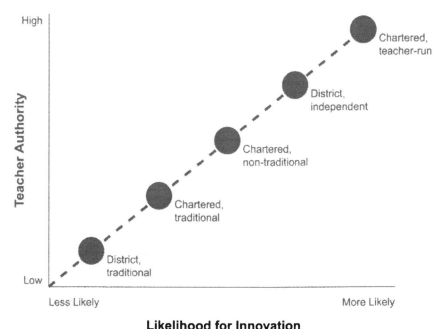

Likelihood for Innovation

Figure 2.1. Axis of innovation

Innovation should increase as teachers are given more authority to design and operate learning programs. District schools could innovate but are not likely to do so, because they have low levels of teacher authority and low capacity for variability.

Traditionally organized schools created by charter would also be less likely to be innovative. The charter gives the school a larger degree of legal independence, but it is the model of school that has consequence in how it plays out.

Meanwhile, nontraditionally organized chartered schools would be inherently more innovative, by virtue of being a different model. The degree to which they rethink learning depends on the school.

District Site-Governed Schools as created by 2009 legislation in Minnesota, or Boston's Pilot Schools, would be more likely to be innovative because they grant teachers more authority.

Schools created by charter that are run by teachers—teacher professional partnerships—would be the most likely to be innovative because they grant teachers maximum authority. Teacher-run schools tend to be more responsive to changes and more efficient than any other arrangement.

Competition

Contract for School Management and Online Education

As schools and districts are cutting the arts, languages, and specialty subjects, online providers are growing in the scope and quality of their offerings. Contracting allows schools to buy online courses as they need them from established universities, nonprofits, and businesses that deliver higher quality at a lower price. *Really? Evidence*

Meanwhile, district boards may use competitive contracting to secure different high-performing organizations to manage their innovative schools, fitting the right management with the right school design. This allows boards of education to receive bids on not only the cost of running schools but also the form they will take. Los Angeles began this process in 2010 for up to a quarter of its schools.

Part Two

THE CURRENT SYSTEM OF K–12 IS NOT SUSTAINABLE

The system of K–12 schooling in the United States, particularly the traditional American high school, is no longer financially viable. There is a structural imbalance in its financing, as costs have been rising faster than growth in revenue and will continue to do so. The factory model of school is subjected to disproportionate cost inflation. At 4–8 percent annually, the price of operating these schools outpaces economic growth and the Consumer Price Index (CPI) year after year.

And there is a productivity paradox, making it very difficult to neutralize inflationary pressures through more efficient production. The

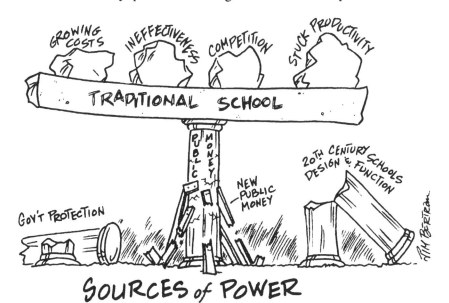

Funding is overwhelmed.

pedagogy of the traditional factory-style school is teacher-driven, and the productivity of a teaching-centered model is limited to the physical capacity of the paid professional. In this setting, productivity can only be improved by increasing class sizes (undesirable) or hiring more teachers (prohibitively expensive).

Meanwhile, performance is stagnant. The traditional school is unable to differentiate pace, content, or type of learning. The mode of production is batch process, necessitating uniformity. And with few exceptions, uniformity *is* mediocrity.

With productivity stuck and costs rising, schools are growing less and less efficient by the year—and a poorer and poorer value to the country. For many years political leaders and education administrators reconciled the structural imbalance through cuts in services and additional spending. That is no longer possible. The system has now hit a wall.

For the first time in a century, there is no new money for K–12. The stimulus is done. Facing increasing pressure from other areas of public spending, it is possible that K–12 may not see another increase in real spending for a very long time. Yet the structural imbalance remains. Costs will continue to increase at more than 4 to 8 percent, year upon year. Schools cannot cut their way to viability. The breaking point is upon us.

Fortunately, there is a third way.

Chapter Three

There Is a Productivity
Paradox in K–12 Education

The cost of running public education is growing faster than available revenues, placing relentless and growing pressures on local and state budgets. Schools and school districts have been experiencing this for decades, paring down their offerings activity by activity, section by section, and course by course in a long, slow, and painful dismantling of the comprehensive middle and secondary school.

For decades school and district administrators have been managing pressured budgets. And it is painful. More and more levies are being brought to the public not for capital investments, but to subsidize basic operations. The referenda are not guaranteed and often fail. Increasingly foundations are turning away from underwriting business as usual, putting school leaders on notice that they want to see change in how things are done.

There are some important cost drivers. Compensation matters, and spending on medical benefits matters. To a lesser extent energy matters, and transportation, and maintenance of infrastructure. There is pressure in labor-intensive industries like teaching to keep increase in compensation on pace with the rate of growth in compensation of other sectors of the economy. There is a problem here, though: In other industries increased pay is driven by improved performance and productivity—something that has not occurred in schooling.

Compensation rises more each year than funding, so it has to be offset by decreases in noncompensation spending or by eliminating positions. The result is constant cuts. While the Great Recession of 2008 onward led to a 1.4 percent decline in the CPI from 2009 to 2010, in Minnesota the average teacher salary increased 4–6 percent (the increase in state appropriation was 2 percent). Paul Hill and Marguerite Roza at the Center for Reinventing Public Education have found that during the same time in New York, teacher salaries increased an average of 5.6 percent.[11] In the ten years from 2000 through 2010, average teacher salaries in the United States increased 30.5 percent. These increases have a significant effect on local and state budgets and on the cost of school.

At the same time, medical costs are growing at three to four times the rate of inflation, compounding the pressure from regular compensation. In New York, costs tied to health benefits rose by 5.1 percent from 2009 to 2010. Hill and Roza figure that health and pension costs alone will drive compensation faster than inflation; taken together, costs of benefits rose from 25 percent of compensation in 1999 to 32 percent in 2006.

National expenditures on K–12 had a compound annual growth rate of 3.72 percent from 1990 through the beginning of the recession in 2008. That was about one and a half times the rate of economic growth, at 2.59 percent.

For those twenty years, as in the decades before, state and local governments met the growing expenditures with added spending. By 2008 it started to become apparent that this trend, like the housing bubble, could not be maintained. There was an economic contraction, so available money actually decreased in real terms. Backsliding budgets were buttressed by debt financing by the federal government, but as the country emerged from the stimulus funding the unsustainable cost-growth was still there.

Over the long term we can hope the economy grows at a faster rate to meet the escalating costs. But hope is not a strategy, and any additional revenue will be met with growing claims from other legitimate areas of public spending: health care, pensions, post-secondary education, servicing of debt. Understand: The core of the problem — mis-designed schools, mis-designed policy, and an underproductive system — has not been resolved. This will take more purposeful work.

State legislators will be on the front lines of decisions in the coming years about how to finance the system. School management will be on the front lines of deciding how to deliver the service.

Managers of traditional schools tend to tighten control in times of financial crisis. Rarely do the administrators of the system reimagine how things are done. Factory schools ratchet up in good times and exercise

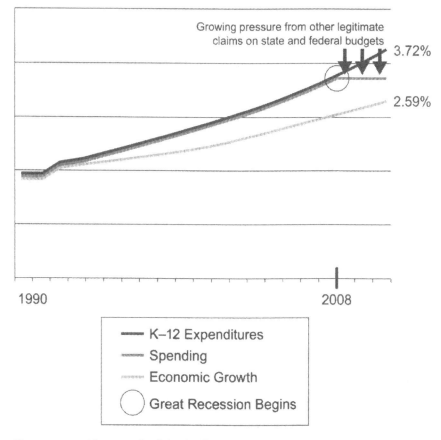

Figure 3.1.   **Without productivity, inefficiency grows**

austerity in the bad—but they tend to not change form. Meanwhile where schools have independence, where teachers are given more professional control, entirely different behavior emerges. There is dynamism, innovation, and creative energy—traits notably missing from the command-and-control system.

The costs of infrastructure and maintenance for district schools are felt through their inverse relationship with declining student enrollment. Many districts are reluctant to sublease excess space to chartered or private schools. As the amount of physical overhead for a shrinking district grows heavier, their spending on instruction wanes.

Meanwhile test scores are flat, graduation rates remain poor, and achievement gaps persist. Despite dramatic growth over the past 30 years in the number of paid adults per student, added programs, and increased spending, National Assessment of Educational Progress (NAEP) performance has remained unchanged.

Traditional factory-style school buildings limit the ability of schools to evolve. News media has moved from print to online. Communications have shed their wires, and computers have migrated from the floor to desktops to handheld. One of the major inhibitors to improvement of school performance, lowering the cost of operation, and proper application of information technology (IT) is the inflexibility of school design.

While performance is stagnant and costs grow, the system becomes more and more inefficient. America's schools will spend more resources this year to achieve the same amount of return as last, as was the prior year's experience and the year before that.

But while rising compensation, health care, and maintenance costs have made conventional public schools financially unsustainable, they are not the taproot. Instead, the problem is that when faced with rising costs, schools have not been able to respond with a commensurate increase in productivity.

The factory model of school—the uniform, course-and-class, batch-process model of traditional schools—is designed to be cost-increasing. Absent serious competition from alternative models, any additional

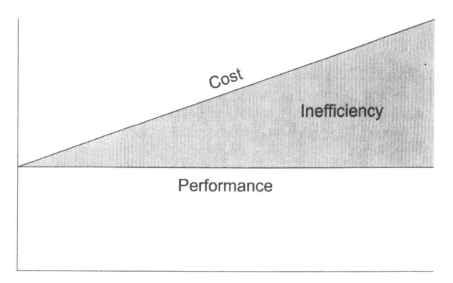

Figure 3.2. Costs are rising faster than growth

costs incurred by factory schools have been seen as necessary, accepted as the price of running a school. The incentives act to encourage cost-generating activity, adding on or bulking up when possible, paring down when needed—but neither in up times nor down are school leaders encouraged to rethink how they do things, to get better value by doing them differently.

This has been the worst possible arrangement for such an important public good, subjecting it to the relentless corrosion of inflation and the dynamism of a changing world, without providing the capability to respond.

LABOR-INTENSIVE INDUSTRIES ARE SUBJECT TO DISPROPORTIONATE COST INFLATION

Looking at those industries where improvements in productivity have been difficult to attain, Clayton Christensen of the Harvard Business School has found that most are labor-intensive and that their built-in inflation rate is 6 to 8 percent. In postal delivery, for example, cost inflation is regularly 7 percent. The inflation rate of household help is 8 percent. In K–12 and higher education, it ranges from 6 to 10 percent.

In each of these industries, Christensen observes that it is difficult to make individual workers more productive. "In most companies the employees get paid 6–8 percent more per year," he told a group in 2005, "but in those where individual employees (aided by improvements in technology) become more productive, the inflation in the cost of the products they ship is only 2–3 percent."[12]

While quality improves, increased productivity holds the price down. The average citizen in the United States is much wealthier today than 30 years ago because advancements in goods and services were matched by improvements in the productivity of business.

The strategy of K–12 to counter inflation has not been to improve productivity but to grow revenue. At some point the bounty ends. When growth in revenue is not sufficient to meet costs, decision makers cut. The tactics of the past 20 years have been to grow and cut. When the capacity to grow revenue is tapped out, unless there is already a process and culture at work to innovate to find new ways of doing things, schools hit a wall.

They are left with no options and all they can do is cut, consolidate, and cut again. That is where we are now.

Thus there will never be "enough" money for the present system. No matter what we do, no matter how much is put in, there never will be enough money. Upwards of 80 percent of expenditures go to compensation. Each budget cycle the number the state allocates for schooling goes onto the table. Then many different bargaining units go after it. At the local level districts cannot take a strike, so they are under strong incentive to settle for more than they have.

There is a settlement, which may not be large itself but more than the 1 to 2 percent increase in state allocation. If additional money cannot be raised, there is a reduction, either in staff numbers or in non-personnel spending.

It is not sufficient to hold schooling harmless on funding cuts. Spending can be held constant but schools are still losing ground, being eaten away by inflating costs. The paradox for education is that within the traditional teacher-lecture arrangement the only way to improve productivity is to assign more students per employee. But if we are going to improve the quality of education, the opposite needs to occur: Learning must become much more personalized. It is a paradox, but it is solvable.

THERE IS A STRUCTURAL IMBALANCE
IN THE COST OF THE SYSTEM

While this productivity paradox means K–12 is becoming more and more inefficient, that alone does not cause the system to be financially unsustainable. The productivity problem has been around for years, but leaders have found ways to cut it down and raise revenues to bring the budgets into line.

The unsustainable reality is the result of a structural imbalance in the cost of schools. A structural imbalance occurs when the costs of running an operation are larger than the amount of money available to fund it, and when costs are projected to grow at a rate faster than new revenue will become available.

"At times the economy grew enough to keep things from caving in," a former state official has said privately, "and other times shifts, income tax surcharges, and such were employed. Nobody worried too much about the structural imbalance. We all figured we could grow our way out of it." Most of those people are still around, he observed, and are only slowly coming to realize that this time it seems different.

Minnesota provides a clear example. In that state, the Office of Management and Budget has projected spending on K–12 to grow at 4.8 percent annually through 2033—two and a half times faster than the projected 2 percent growth of the CPI.[13]

Meanwhile, costs across the state government are expected to grow on aggregate at 5.4 percent, compounding the pressures on schools by creating a structural imbalance in the state budget generally. This is driven by demographic pressures on entitlements and medical and hospital services, and it is reflective of the situation in states throughout the country.

The structural imbalance of state budgets means that K–12 will be competing for fewer relative dollars while its own financial base erodes. There are other pressures that policymakers must respond to. Public education cannot wait for the cost pressures to abate or for more money to come in.

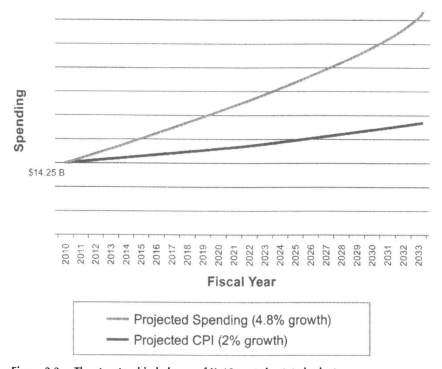

Figure 3.3. The structural imbalance of K–12 costs in state budgets

The structural imbalance is not going to resolve itself. Not only are costs rising, but revenues are politically constrained. State appropriations must be voted on in competition now with those growing claims from medical and social services. Baby boomer retirement and health care costs will couple with a decrease in their taxable income and spending. Citizens are calling for an expensive renaissance in transit, with local and interstate high-speed rail. Local levies are fixed or are difficult to raise through referendum.

Higher costs cannot simply be passed on to users, nor can schools easily adapt to account for changing conditions. If a factory school grows during demographic or economic boons, these pains are exacerbated when trends turn downward. We can't cut one-third of a teacher, can we? Yes

Districts are working to increase state financing. Sometimes they organize campaigns for adequate revenue. Sometimes they sue the state, asking the courts to require the legislature to increase funding. But nothing stops the rise in costs. So the districts never seem to have enough.

In other sectors of the economy, increases in productivity offset the rise in costs. Sometimes a company will rearrange or completely redesign a business model to find new and different ways to do things. In times of change, finding efficiencies while retaining the old model is often not sufficient. There is still performance to consider, and making a school lower-cost (perhaps by cutting services) does not mean it will be more effective.

At these times enterprises must innovate, to get more for the same amount of work or to perform at the same levels with fewer people doing the work.

There is no related concept of productivity right now in education. District and policy leaders see school as financing teaching, not as financing learning. This would be similar to focusing on broadsheets over the news, or focusing on a DVD instead of the movie that goes onto it.

Innovation is often on the table only if it maintains the teaching-centered paradigm. Too often, as Dan Loritz puts it, we protect the church at the expense of the faith. So course offerings are reduced, class sizes grow, and less-able people are hired. By not focusing on learning, the notion that there might be more effective and more efficient ways of doing things passes decision makers right by.

FUNDAMENTALLY, THIS IS
NOT A PROBLEM OF REVENUE

The question of how much money is spent on primary and secondary schooling is separate from the question of how teaching and learning take place. Both are legitimate questions, but they are separate questions. As a nation we have been focusing almost exclusively on more or less services and more or less money.

There is, in fact, an enormous amount of money in America's K–12 system—over half a trillion dollars. The problem of the structural imbalance of K–12 financing is not one of resources, but of productivity—and that in turn is a problem with the design of schools and school systems.

We have an underproductive education system in the United States, and this shows in its rising costs. For example, a school may do one year precisely what it did the year prior—offer the same courses, with the same faculty teaching the same load, spending the same on operations and maintenance. It may enroll the same number of students and receive the same allocation per pupil and identical supplementary funds as the year before.

In this case, the level of service would remain constant. Yet while the school maintains its operations, the cost of those services are rolling ahead from one year to the next at +2, +4, or +8 percent. Meanwhile, the world progresses. Our complacency is quickly exposed to erosion, both economically and academically.

If costs continue to rise faster than revenues, then two options become immediately apparent. The first is to increase the budget of schools by 6–8 percent each year, year after year, either by raising revenue through economic growth or by levying new taxes. Both are tricky propositions and come with no guarantee that they will work.

The second option is to decrease the amount of services delivered by 4–6 percent, year after year, to account for the difference in inflation and an estimated 2 percent rise in the CPI. For years schools have been choosing the latter, slowly cutting programs and offerings, searching for efficiencies, and laying off staff. The result has been tumult, and strained relations within and among schools, districts, statehouses, and the public.

While it is insufficient to hold schools harmless on spending cuts, it is also not fair. Other public spending areas with serious and legitimate claims for the public good—medical and hospital services, welfare, post-secondary education, infrastructure, economic development—are experiencing increased pressure because of the preferred status of schooling.

THERE IS ANOTHER WAY—TARGETING PRODUCTIVITY

Innovation is the way that organizations and systems stay relevant and viable in times of change. It is the process that uncovers new and better ways to do things, finding new ways of combining advancements in technology with alternative business models of school.

The core of the cost and performance problems of schooling is unchanging performance for a rising price. Yet it is possible now to radically customize learning in ways that could not be done just a few years ago. Schools can be redesigned to better facilitate personalization and to improve the cost and operations of the organization. To do this the country needs to embark on a strategy of innovation that rethinks some of our core assumptions about how schooling is arranged and functions.

For example, we can be getting much more than we are from students and from teachers. The factory school is unable to differentiate pace or content, and so tends to the lowest common denominator. This is a motivation killer, and an artificial limiter on the effort that may be put forth even if a student is ready and willing. Productivity is capped at the capacity of the teacher to present information and engage students. In this model, productivity is improved by adding students to a teacher's load, and costs are decreased by employing fewer professionals.

Today, in the information age, there are three new ways to improve the productivity of schools: increase teacher load by moving online, increase student labor through technology-mediated learning, and design learning models that can run at a lower cost. *— what does this mean?*

First, online learning (as it is now and is evolving) has significant capacity to improve productivity. Teachers online can handle up to twice the student load than in a conventional bricks-and-mortar classroom. By accessing material themselves, students can move at their own pace and communicate more with each other and with the teacher than is often the case in the traditional setting.

Not yet it isn't.

The quality of online learning has increased rapidly, and will into the future. Not only do the technologies continue to march ahead, but the culture of youth is changing as well. It is far more natural for a 15-year-old to learn virtually today than it was even 10 years ago.

There is evidence that for many students the experience online may be *Depends on the child.* significantly better than in a classroom. The U.S. Department of Education commissioned a literature review of studies on online learning, published in 2009. It found that in terms of student engagement, "blended" classroom/online learning turned out to be the most effective, followed by online learning and last, by the traditional classroom.[14]

Online learning is adaptable. Students can adapt it to their needs, enrolling in a single specialty course from a college or business, learning a language from a student/tutor program, or taking an entire load of courses all at once or knocking them down one after another, in close order.

The second way to improve productive, technology-mediated learning is using learning management systems or intelligent tutoring software to make students the drivers of learning. *Vague*

Student labor is a tremendously underused resource in schools. Modern technologies can engage students and move school from teaching-centered to learning-centered. Since the use of student labor in traditional schools is very low, the potential is significant. Putting a classroom of students to work can quickly multiply the net labor in a classroom without any increase in compensation costs. *Not really showing how*

Finally, it is possible to design schools that run at a much lower cost than large factory schools. These are appearing across the country, and those that are able to combine a lower operating cost with better productivity constitute a sort of "super model" of school that was outlined and discussed at length in chapter 1.

CAST SCHOOLING IN TERMS OF VALUE

The factory school and the command-and-control regulatory framework that oversees it is an unnecessarily poor value. The results per dollar in public education are not what they could be—and they are trending in the wrong direction. The structural imbalance means that while public schools are growing less and less efficient, they are also becoming a poorer and poorer value to the taxpayer.

What is worse is that the factory model is organizationally incapable of significantly increasing its value. This is the productivity paradox: While the costs for public schools roll forward higher each year, they are becoming neither more effective nor more efficient. So the value drops.

And the country is sick of it. They may not always know the cause, but the public understands something is wrong with this deal. They see that legislatures and others continue to pour money into this thing, but no qualitative leaps have been made. If anything, there has been decline—in courses offered, in extracurricular activities, and in global standing.

Unsub stantiated!

The notion of value cannot be overlooked. It is central to everything. It is at the root of growing popular discontent about public education and its professionals, and it is the only way that the system can pull out of its downward slide. Figure out how to improve value, and you have got it.

Taxpayers and philanthropists will be more willing to fund increases in the cost of schools if they feel the value is improving. This means a reduction in the cost structure, better productivity, and a significant increase in performance. With the right strategy, this can be done.

Optimization

Supplement Teachers with Retirees Willing to Serve

There is tremendous opportunity to increase the adult-student ratio in schools without hiring additional full-time, highly trained teachers.

Perhaps the largest untapped resource are retirees, of which there will be a larger proportion in coming years. Schools can make use of veteran teachers who are retiring with 10–25 good working years ahead of them and a desire to contribute. The primary opportunity for these highly capable and experienced retirees to stay involved now is to be a substitute teacher.

Invite these veterans in, let them keep their pension, and pay by the hour. They can be teacher-coaches, teaching aids, mentors, curriculum developers, and extracurricular support. These roles may be more easily included in school models that provide authority to the teachers and management to be flexible in their staffing and decision making.

Oh I see. So a solution to get experienced people to work cheaply!

Chapter Four

Redesigning Schools for Performance

The traditional factory model of middle and high school is an inhibited business model. Without its preferred status in public affairs, many traditional public schools would have evolved or folded long ago. We are shifting away from factory-model schools, which most Americans grew up with, and the push for change is being driven entirely by family demand.

The people inside schools are the system's most underused resources. For students, the problem is wasted time and low motivation. There is tremendous potential in students who are bored, alienated, suppressed, oppressed, or otherwise disconnected from the process. For teachers, it is the drag of a job that is constrained and not treated with appropriate professional dignity. The inefficiencies in public education occur in five areas.

1. Decision Making

The perennial dissonance and grinding between school leadership and the staff is itself a serious inefficiency. One unwise authoritarian decision, while quick at the time, can lead to months or years of inefficiency resulting from angst and difficulty of implementation.

Decisions over spending, operations, and structure are removed from those who carry them out, missing the opportunity to employ the creative capacities of staff and removing many natural incentives for saving money and improving practice. The distance between those who make decisions and the teachers who carry them out decreases ownership of the school's direction and accountability for results.

2. Discipline and School Culture

When the authority for discipline is assumed by a single administrator or administrative team, discipline is often less efficient or effective. Students know when teachers do or do not have control, and they understand where the authority ultimately rests. To the student, the office is the only place that really matters, and that makes the job more difficult for the teacher and inhibits the school culture.

By contrast, where teachers run a school collectively or share authority with the principal, problems of discipline and decorum can drop sharply. High School for Recording Arts (HSRA) in Saint Paul enrolls a majority of male African American students, almost all returning to school after having first dropped out or been kicked out of traditional schools. They are a hard lot. Yet decorum surpasses that of most suburban high schools. Staff treat the students more like adults at work than children to subordinate. All teachers are responsible for all learners. One staff member is tasked with floating the school, helping with projects, and seeking and ironing out social wrinkles before they become problems.

The organizational culture in factory schools is poor. In the model of shared authority, many would-be problems of decorum and culture just do not occur. Not only is time and energy saved that would otherwise have gone to maintaining order, but student-teacher relationships improve and the academic atmosphere is less interrupted.

3. Spending

The closer to the classroom that decisions over spending are made, the more effective and efficient they tend to be. Creativity flows for finding spending alternatives, and staff get involved in innovating to save money and to do more with less. In the right conditions teachers are better at identifying needs and channeling resources than central administrators and central planners.

One major district confronted an interesting challenge when teachers began putting together proposals for their own in-district, teacher-run schools. The teachers began to ask why it was that 15–20 percent of their money was not passed through from its public and private sources, but instead held back by the central office.

"We don't know," came the reply. The administrators just did not know where that money went. And not for lack of talent: They had recently hired some of the best finance staff anywhere. Somewhere, somehow, it got sucked up by the central office. This is not unique—clarity of decisions and spending is a challenge of large districts throughout the country.

One city district, Minneapolis Public Schools (MPS), spent $19,625 per student. Meanwhile a project-based, teacher-run high school in the Twin Cities—one of the best-performing high schools in the state—spent $9,780 per student.[15]

This too is not unique to MPS; it is a problem common to the traditional system. Between the sources of revenue and the schools there is an organization with authority over the schools and their funds. This is an efficiency problem, because the central office is not well positioned to make spending decisions in schools and has the incentive and authority to withhold for its own programs. Unless given control over how money is spent, schools have neither the ability nor incentive to do things differently to save resources.

4. Use of Staff

In traditional schools teachers are often not able to explore alternative methods or create new learning models. They have much to contribute.

A leader at a teacher-run school put it this way: "Teachers have all of these untapped skills. Within any school I'll bet you could go and find among the teachers somebody who would be interested in the budget; somebody would be interested in personnel and human resources; somebody would be interested in marketing; somebody would be interested in analyzing test data. I think a lot of large school districts don't tap those resources of what's already in the building. And relying on one person, an administrator, to do all of those things may not be the most efficient use of resources."[16]

5. Use of Student Labor

Young people could be giving much more than they are. They could be contributing to the work of school, instead of sitting idle. Students may be motivated to pursue a particular subject or skill, but do not have the opportunity or incentive.

Good idea, but does not necessarily use less resources.

Mastery Learning by another names

Schools should be arranged around learning, not teaching. Make students do more of the laboring in pursuit of knowledge, enabled by IT. Allow them to progress quickly in some areas and more slowly in others, judging by their ability to demonstrate mastery of material.

MOTIVATION IS CENTRAL

Motivation is at the root of effective teaching and learning. When Ted Kolderie talks about it he walks the logic out: If learning matters, then effort matters. And if effort matters, then motivation, more than any other factor, is the driver for both teacher and student.

Teachers are told what to do and how to do it, and they are excluded from the decision making about how their school is organized and run. Teachers are tenured but have little actual control. This removes much of their professional and creative license.

Students have even less control; they are confined to desks and marched class to class, course to course, and grade to grade, at the same pace.

School design ought to be shaped around student and teacher motivation, to maximize interest and effort. But even with the greatest of effort, coaxed or forced, there is only so much a teacher can do within the bounds of the factory school.

Conventional thought in education has been that to make better use of scarce resources, administrators need to get teachers to work harder. Standards, assessments, and merit pay are efforts at this. The capacity of these tools to improve teaching and learning are fundamentally constrained by the parameters of school design.

There is little capacity for variability in the factory school. And without variability, it is rigid. Progress needs variability to get to the way schools work, to incorporate developments in modern information technologies.

NEW ELECTRONICS ARE DIFFICULT
TO APPLY IN THE OLD SCHOOL MODEL

Despite good efforts and good intentions, electronics have been undereffective at moving the needle on student performance. Digital electronics have simply been added on to the existing models of school instead of being allowed to remake them from the ground up.

Larry Cuban framed it right when he said that computers are "oversold and underused."[17] While IT is ubiquitous in the lives of young people, computers and other electronics remain relegated to classroom walls. The dichotomy between IT use in a student's private and school lives is dramatic—yet it is predictable. The wallflower is often the primary role for electronics to play in a school model where teacher-lecture is the necessary pedagogy.

In the traditional school, electronics are frequently distractions as much as learning aids. Students want to be using the electronics for a type of application that does not work in the factory model. The inability to rethink school operating models in conjunction with the adoption of electronics is the core reason why K–12 has failed to reap the benefits of the IT revolution.

THE CHARACTER OF THE TRADITIONAL SCHOOL AND SYSTEM IS STATIC

The mass production model of education is essentially the same today as it was 100 years ago. It has several features:

- School is defined in time, in space, and in its form of organization. A traditional school is a building to which children come for certain years of their lives, months of the year, days of the week, and hours of the day. There they are grouped by age into grades, to be instructed by adults.
- The school itself is not a discrete organization but a unit of a larger organization that owns its facility, employs its teachers, provides its revenue, and sets out its method of operation and designs its curriculum. The teachers, unlike professionals in many other white-collar occupations, are not in charge of the administrators but work for the administrators.
- Schooling, the process of learning, is conceived of as instruction. Learning is thought of as the effect of teaching. It is quite common to hear people talk about "delivering education." School is designed around the adult, not the student. Young people sit in desks, in rows, while an adult

imparts knowledge. There is limited, if any, opportunity for customization or personalization of the learning process. Student interests are treated as largely irrelevant to what "has" to be taught.

- The assumption is that all students will know all subjects. Secondary students are tested mainly on their ability to recall factual knowledge. Success is defined as scoring well on tests for that knowledge, most involving testing for discrete, right-or-wrong answers.

Or former ground here

Conventional school is like a school bus rolling along the highway, with the teacher standing at the front and pointing out interesting and important sights but telling the passengers that, no, we cannot let you get off to explore what's down that side road. Students who want to pursue their interests and passions must do so on their own time and energy, if they have any left.

This batch processing in education has obvious limitations. It requires all students in the class to proceed through the full term and at the same pace, affording little opportunity for those who need more time to take more time and little opportunity for those who could move faster to move faster. In the typical mixed-ability classroom, this confronts the teacher with a difficult, almost impossible, task.

Moreover, educational course and content requirements too often tie the hands of students who want to pursue different or more sophisticated curricula. Four years of English are not inherently superior to two years of English and two years of philosophy or two years of journalism, but in almost no American high school today does the student have a choice.

Traditional schools do not easily permit students who develop a particular interest to pursue that interest, no matter how strong the motivation or how useful the learning that might result. The pursuit of individual interests has become even harder as states have added more and more required courses to the high school curriculum, slowly squeezing out electives.

Alternatives sometimes exist for special-needs students and for those "not doing well," but the batch production model of education makes addressing the needs of these students expensive and still not very customized. For mainstream students and more talented students, there is not much in the way of alternatives.

Is it any wonder then that so many young people drop out, with many of the students who stay doing so only because they need the formality of the high school diploma? Yet we carry forward almost unquestioned a batch processing model of school and teaching not designed to motivate either students or teachers. Instead of innovating to find new approaches, we try to improve performance by pushing ever harder to standardize and perfect the old technology of textbook and teacher instruction.

America's factory-school model was a rational and purposeful result of the technology of instruction that existed at its creation. It reflects the economics of scarcity that until quite recently imposed themselves not just on information industries (film, music, television, books, newspapers, magazines) but on most industries. Until the IT revolution it was not economically feasible to produce customized products or services.

In the old economy, scale was essential. The old economy was a mass production economy where the underlying technology system limited product and service diversity. Changing factory-floor production technology usually took skilled labor many days or even weeks. Dedicated machines that could only do one thing—stamp out a particular car door—had to be taken down and replaced with a new one that could do something different. The situation was not much different in offices. Changing software on mainframe computers required software engineers to reprogram complex and expensive proprietary software systems.

The education sector paralleled other sectors of the old economy. It was not economically feasible to provide a teacher for every child, to place a set of encyclopedias in every home, to provide a unique textbook for each student, or to erect a high school in every neighborhood. Thus school developed as a place to which students came to be grouped into classes and instructed together with the same texts before moving on to the next phase of the production process—their next class. And because the adult and books were the only sources of information for youth, the only possible pedagogy was teacher-led, uniform instruction.

"It must have been an act of God," Joe Graba says, "that made all courses take the same amount of time as each other, and for all students to learn at the same pace."

"It was designed to last, and it is lasting," complained a liberal Democratic state senate leader in 2010.[18]

The factory model served its purpose brilliantly in the 20th century, getting students into desks and equalizing access and quality. The system achieved this by running the assembly line. The problem is that if we want higher performance from students, we are going to need to break up the uniformity and allow the system to be responsible to individuals. But customization in the factory model is prohibitively expensive.

It is very costly, for example, to put a student on an Individual Education Program (IEP), and so extra public funding is provided for special education. This pays for extra time spent by staff and for hiring specialists. More and more students are being classified as special education, leading to pricier school supplements. There is no way this IEP arrangement can keep growing in factory schools. And herein lies the problem: All students have special needs. The old economy is gone, but we are yet to move into a new age of school design. This has not been for the absence of need, but the absence of strategy.

Deregulation

Decentralize Authority

Productivity and value are improved through innovation, and innovation requires autonomy. Allow teachers to use their position, experience, and expertise to creatively respond to student needs. Give them control of the materials and means of learning, including management of core school functions and operations. Delegate decision making on academics and operations; let teachers decide how students will learn.

Design regulation around the principles of a sound market. Allow for choice and competition. Invite in entrepreneurs. Put in mechanisms for quality control that rely on incentives and voluntary compliance, not command and control and the constant policing that comes with it. Give teachers more professional control so they take ownership over change and begin to drive it.

Such as?, Notoriously hard in education,

Part Three

DESIGN MATTERS

Education leaders need to rethink the ways in which schools involve students, their application of modern technologies, and the forms in which they are managed and regulated. As cost pressures grow and the demand for better performance intensifies, schools need to flip from being teaching-centered and teacher-driven to learning-centered and student-driven.

Productivity improvements occur through the introduction of new technologies. In labor-intensive industries like schooling, it is difficult to make individual workers more productive or efficient. Significant improvements

Design and technology.

in productivity come through the introduction of technologies that enable workers to accomplish tasks better, at a lower relative cost.

Combine innovations in technology with innovations in school models. Modern technologies are insufficient unless paired with the right business model. Adding new technologies to a traditionally organized school increases cost and teacher labor without significantly improving productivity. This is essential. Innovations in technology must be paired with innovations in the business (school) model—with changes driven by the user.

There are three ways to improve productivity in schools: increase teacher load by moving classes online, or "disintermediating" (using technology to pick up tasks the teacher would otherwise have to do); increase student labor through technology-mediated learning; or design lower-cost school models that both run on less money and continually seek ways to improve performance and lower cost.

Performance will follow mass customization, and excellence will take varied forms. Universal standards are by their nature universally low or widely thwarted. Do not confuse high-expectations-for-all with uniformity. Do not conflate equality of opportunity with uniformity. The public school system must be able to accommodate the extra-ordinary, which requires variability. Variability produces plurality, and for some, specialization.

Chapter Five

Redesigning Schools and the Public Schooling System

In the work of improving schools, there are strategies and there are tools. There are symptoms of problems and there are the causes of them. Getting clarity on these distinctions is a necessary first step.

Standards, state and federal testing—these are tools. Poor achievement and strained budgets are symptoms of problems. Most efforts at improvement direct the tools at the symptoms, without much change. What we really need to be doing is targeting the root causes of the problems of performance and cost, and devising strategies that change the conditions that bring them about.

Students are unmotivated. Why are they unmotivated? What is the cause? IT has been scandalously underused and misused in schools across the country. Why is that? Often computers result in more work for the teacher and higher cost for the school. Other electronics are merely distractions. Yet every other information industry has been completely remade by these same technologies. Why not schooling?

By getting past the effects of problems and finding their causes, clarity emerges about how to go about setting a course for improvement. The goal is better policy design, improving schools, and changing behavior by thinking in terms of the systems in which people operate.

SCHOOLS AND THE SYSTEMS NEED TO BE RETHOUGHT

This country cannot resolve the performance and cost problems of public education by cutting programs and spending more. The structural imbalance of costs and revenue means that any cuts now will only be negated

53

as time progresses. Resolution of the imbalance requires the neutralizing of cost drivers or, where that cannot happen, improvements in productivity to offset them.

Ted Kolderie talks about a spectrum of redesign of organizations, from small to large scale. On one end there is performance improvement, through refinement or enhancement of what is already in place. On the other end, he says, there is what Walt McClure calls macro system design or large-system architecture, working to create a system where schools are driven to improve by their own intrinsic desire and motivation (and not require constant "banging" from the outside).[19] This is the realm of those who design policy, such as school boards and state legislatures. (See figure 5.1.)

In the discussions about strained budgets there is talk about cutting, or getting more: more revenue, more effort from the employees, or more capital investment for when times are good. Rarely is there talk about doing things differently. "Everyone wants school to be better," Joe Graba likes to say, "but almost nobody wants it to be different."

At its roots the unsustainable nature of public education, and the intractability of performance, is basically a problem of the design of schools. Problems of cost, performance, and motivation are functions of the design. In order to understand the distinction between symptomatic problems and causal problems, one must first see how public education can be made to work better.

The need to redesign schools can be shown through a set of observations that are increasingly proving true. First, we cannot get the performance we need as a country with the schools we now have. We have been trying this for decades, with no radical change. If we want different results, then we need to do things differently.

Second, people talk of goals but usually not of strategies to achieve those goals. If we continue to talk of "closing the achievement gap," raising graduation rates, or improving math and science scores, we need to understand that these are goals and not strategies.

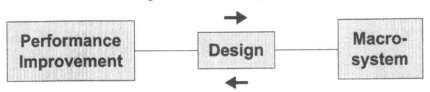

Figure 5.1.   Performance improvement and system design

Third, many initiatives put forth as solutions are not themselves strategies for improving learning. Curriculum, uniform standards, performance-based compensation—these are tools that can help drive changes. But they do not improve learning without a larger, macro-level strategy that involves changes in system dynamics and incentives.

Finally, no systems are permanent, and they must (and can) change with the times.

GET AT THE ROOT OF THE PROBLEMS

In 2009 William Ouchi implored those around schools to think more deeply on what causes the ills in urban education. "Is anyone recommending that General Motors repair itself," he asked as that company came out of bankruptcy, "by retraining its workers, or by adopting performance-based compensation for them?" About the health care debate raging nationally at that time, he asked, "Are people advocating that we solve the nation's health care problems by altering the curriculum in schools of medicine?"[20]

The answer to both questions, he said, is no. "Why, then, does it make sense for us to attack the problems of urban schools with equivalent measures: improving teacher training, adopting merit pay, or changing the curriculum and books?"

We have been firing away at what is visible—what can be seen—and so have been treating the symptoms of a school model that is in fact obsolete.

Political action is compelled to go after symptoms. Policymaking has trouble moving to causes. Symptoms are visible, and it is easy for politicians to point to problems and describe how things should be. An effort to go after causes is harder, takes more time, and inevitably calls into question the institutional arrangements. Stakeholders in the system do not take kindly to proposals that would disrupt the way things are and how they are done.

To avoid major controversy, people in political life usually accept the existing arrangements and work within them. They assume the form and functions of school as a given. This means the challenges in K–12 are defined as *problems of performance* (students and teachers should work harder) and *not as problems of design* (schools must change if their behavior is to change).

ASK THE RIGHT QUESTIONS

Enormous amounts of time, money, and attention are spent chasing answers to questions that do not get at the systemic causes of the problems they seek to solve. Some common examples and better alternatives include the following:

- Not: School needs to become more personalized. How can we afford to hire 50–100 percent more teachers? Instead: How can learning be personalized without hiring more teachers?
- Not: So we have all this technology, but how do we get schools to adopt it? Instead: How can schools be designed so that they want to adopt this technology?
- Not: Why don't students see school as relevant? Instead: What do students want school to do?
- Not: Why don't teachers (and their unions) change? Instead: What is causing their resistance to reform?
- Not: How can schools get adequate funding? Instead: Do we really need to spend as much as we do?
- Not: How can we make the traditional factory school run on 80 percent of its present resources? Instead: How can we design a new school from the ground up so that it requires only 80 percent of the revenue of traditional arrangement?
- Not: How can we get the top tier of college graduates to become teachers? Instead: Why don't those in the top tier want to be teachers? *Pay & Culture*
- Not: How can schools keep students from bringing and using electronics during class? Instead: How can they be incorporated? Relatedly . . .
- Not: Where can electronics be added on to classes? Instead: How can school be redesigned by using technology? *No. What curricula design is best?*
- Not: Why don't students work hard? Instead: How can the dynamic be flipped so that school is learning-driven, not teaching-driven?
- Not: Why can't young people just behave, grow up? Instead: How can schools begin to treat students more like adults? *But they aren't adults.*

The reframing of many of these questions involves a paradigm shift. This is not work that can be done with half-efforts.

INNOVATION IS THE METHOD

If productivity is not improved, public schools will continue to erode. Districts will go bankrupt. Private options will move in from the fringes and begin peeling away students one by one, through new technologies that have a growing appeal in quality, cost, and accessibility.

Not everyone believes innovation is necessary. There is a common thought in education that we now know everything that needs to be known — that it is now just a question of replication and execution. Some very influential people have little appreciation for the changes in school design and learning made possible now by information technologies.

Innovation uncovers all sorts of things we never thought possible — things that often were not possible until a new technology came along and made it so. When the world changes, an organization must change the way it looks at it, responds to it, and prepares for it. Of the 100 most well-capitalized companies in America at the turn of the 20th century, only three were around a century later — and they were substantially different. Public education operates within the same dynamic. It should trouble us that the basic design of school has not changed in generations.

Large organizations have a difficult time innovating unless they de-centralize authority. As innovation increases within a centralized organization, it tires quickly. But as it increases within an operation that is decentralized, it becomes more dynamic and energetic as the creativity and energy of more and more people are brought in.

Table 5.1. Traditional versus Innovative Schools

Traditional	Innovative
Schools large	Schools small
Factory model	Many models
Interdependent architecture	Modular architecture
Community weak	Community strong
Discipline centralized	Discipline shared
Teachers as employees	Teachers as partners
Students controlled	Students guided
School as social-service agency	School as responsive community
Values detached from learning	Values core to the learning model
Irrelevant	Relevant
Structurally resistant to change	Self-improving

Spreading innovation around makes sense. It is more effective and efficient to have 1,000 people working on a problem than 10. It puts to work the excess capacity and creativity of teachers and volunteers in a community. Those closer to the students know better what they need and would respond well to. Others can play important roles developing alternative modes of assessment, aiding entrepreneurship, and conducting research that analyzes the peculiarities of new models.

Innovation happens on the edges of what is known. It involves trying new things. Replication, while appropriate and necessary, is not innovation. Pushback is gathering against the notion of trying new things, with people saying that schools should just "take what works." Some of this is risk aversion, and some is hubris. With care, public policy can minimize the likelihood of failures without hampering creativity. But some degree of trial and error is required. Knowledge does not precede experience, but follows it.

INTERDEPENDENCIES MAKE CHANGE DIFFICULT

The components of the established system are mutually reinforcing, from the roles of management and labor to the formulas for funding and the schedules of busing. Clayton Christensen asserts that "the economics of an interdependent system oblige standardization."[21] With colleagues Michael Horn and Curt Johnson, he has identified four forms of interdependencies in the factory school arrangement.

First, *temporal interdependencies* necessitate the uniform pacing of instruction. A student cannot study something in 8th grade until he or she passes through 7th grade.

Second are *lateral interdependencies*, or consistencies in the way things are taught. "The way we teach foreign language grammar in high school could be better," Horn has said, "but to teach that we'd have to redesign how we teach English grammar in the early years, which would require a fundamental change in the reading program."[22]

Third, *physical interdependencies* premised on facilities severely limit what sorts of innovations may take place. "Project-based learning has been shown to be better for many students, but our schools are designed in such a way as to prevent it." who is this quote from?

Last, there are *hierarchical interdependencies*, or top-down require-ments and restrictions on what a teacher can do. Once requirements and regulations from the state, local, and federal levels are all accounted for, teachers end up quite constrained.

The alternative is modularity, rearranging the system so that each of its components may move with more independence of the others. In this environment, the best role for central administration is less command-and-control than coordination.

The goal of policy should be to design a framework that gives those on the front line the most possible control, channeling their energies and insights with incentives that drive them toward continual self-diagnosis and improve-ment. The alternative is to direct a field of automatons. Considering what all people can contribute if given the chance, that is the height of inefficiency.

FOCUS ON SCHOOL PROCESSES,
NOT INPUTS AND OUTPUTS

Ted Kolderie illustrates the concept of design work with a processor. On one end are the inputs to the box, or money and labor. On the other end are the outputs, such as the graduates and the programs a school is able to offer.

Most popular and political attention has focused only on these two components: money in, statistics out. Wanting improvement, discussion leaps from the inputs of the system right to its outputs. There are demands

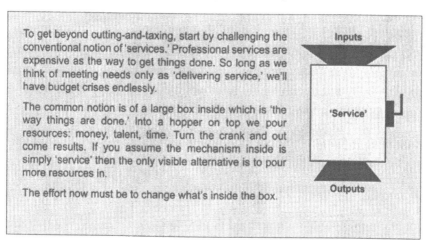

To get beyond cutting-and-taxing, start by challenging the conventional notion of 'services.' Professional services are expensive as the way to get things done. So long as we think of meeting needs only as 'delivering service,' we'll have budget crises endlessly.

The common notion is of a large box inside which is 'the way things are done.' Into a hopper on top we pour resources: money, talent, time. Turn the crank and out come results. If you assume the mechanism inside is simply 'service' then the only visible alternative is to pour more resources in.

The effort now must be to change what's inside the box.

Inputs

'Service'

Outputs

Figure 5.2. Rethinking "how"

for greater effectiveness and calls for accountability. Policymakers set standards, figuring people will find ways to meet them.

Many people want to get more without seriously changing how we do it. But what matters for school behavior is what transpires to provide the result we see. It is what goes inside the box that counts.

Schools and school districts are visible by their physical aspects: the buildings, their fields, and the bright yellow school buses darting across town. But more than anything else they are comprised of and driven by people: students, teachers, staff, administrators, the public. The system is how policymakers and state officials have chosen to organize these individuals into roles; house and fund them; assign responsibilities; and reward, punish, or compel their action.

It is difficult for a layperson to understand the workings of the system, let alone advocate change for it. There are many laws, rules, and jargon. There are professionals and there are experts, and they have done a good job setting up boundaries around their work.

When things became convoluted, C.S. Lewis would step back and ask, "What is this thing's (this system's) basic function?"[23] It is easy to think that public school is something only the expert managers can handle. But do not confuse the goals society has with the present character of the system.

Unless the buildings, the fields, and the buses are effectively moving toward the goals we have for K–12, all the particulars of the system are meaningless. The board meetings, conferences, and negotiations are "simply a waste of time," as Lewis would say. Why not do something different?

The traditional system passes students from grade to grade without regard to whether they learn or not. And if a student does not learn, the schools do not actually have a strategy to address the problem. They have no process to decipher what the particular problem is for an individual student. They do not rethink the processes the student goes through day to day—the processes that brings the result—because they cannot change it anyhow. So they move on. Scarce resources are directed elsewhere.

DESIGN BEGETS INCENTIVES

People in organizations small and large operate inside a collection of dynamics that, knowingly or unknowingly, influence the sorts of decisions they make and the ways in which they work.

Table 5.2. Old versus New Models of Schooling and Learning

Old Model	New Model
Reform existing schools	Create new schools
Larger schools	Smaller schools
"Delivering education"	Students learning
Read books; listen to talk	Explore the Web
Time-bound and place-bound	Any time and any place
Technology as textbook	Technology for research
Groups and classes	Individualized
Time is fixed	Time is variable
Standardization	Customization
Cover material	Understand key ideas
Who and what	Why and how
Know things	Apply knowledge
Tradition	Relevance
Multiple-choice tests	Written/oral demonstrations
Testing for accountability	Testing for understanding
"Make 'em"	"Motivate 'em"
Instructors	Advisers/facilitators
Teachers serve administrators	Administrators serve teachers
Administrative management	Professional partnership
Adult interests dominate	Student interests dominate

The people involved in American school systems—the teachers, administrators, staff, and students—are exceptionally diverse, more diverse than anywhere else in the world. Yet despite this diversity certain behaviors can be observed that are consistent across districts large and small; rural, suburban, and urban schools; and people of all ages, races, and backgrounds.

It is standard for teachers and administrators to view each other with skepticism if not downright contempt. Students are checked out. One-third do not graduate, and another one in five say they are merely checking the box until they can move on into the next stage. The apathy and discontent with public education has become a part of the popular consciousness, tying together generations and people of all backgrounds.

That the same behavior is occurring across the country, with so many different people in such varied conditions, indicates there is something larger at work here, something in the particulars of the system that is causing the similarity in behavior. There must be some good or bad incentives, rules, and regulations that are acting upon people to drive them all toward the same behavior.

This is less a question of the individuals, then, because all people good or bad are subject to the same dynamics. Instead it is systematic. What is it about the system that causes this collective behavior?

Incentive = Reason + Opportunity (money, ability, authority)

Figure 5.3.   The composition of an incentive

INCENTIVES AFFECT BEHAVIOR

Incentives are the coming together of reason and opportunity. If the fundamentals of a system are aligned right, improvement happens. Incentives encourage and reward the right kind of behavior and dissuade the wrong kind. People in the system are able to do good and resist doing bad.

Many students and teachers do not have adequate incentives to work hard, because either the reason is unclear or they do not have proper outlets for adding efforts. In a model that moves students through courses and classes at the same pace, a bright young person seeking admittance to an elite college may have reason to move quickly—but does he or she have the opportunity?

Incentives are derived from laws and regulations. Education policies are commonly discussed in terms of the goals they proclaim rather than the incentives or opportunities they create. Incentives have the ability to defeat the objectives of policy. Bright people and good intentions are regularly overridden by counterincentives: A teacher is unable to get students interested; principals struggle to get the teachers to be proactive in cooperating; state and federal regulators are frustrated at their inability to change the performance of schools by assessing them and adding or subtracting funding.

"Systems of people behave the way they are structured and rewarded to behave," Walt McClure says. "Poor structure tends to beget poor incentives, and poor incentives tend to beget poor performance. If we desire improved performance . . . we must improve its structure and incentives."[24]

Identify the fundamental incentives from which all others derive. Get to the source. Change there can affect everything else down the line. Put teachers in charge of a budget, for example, and let them keep for the school what they do not spend. Expenditures will drop. The whole game changes.

HAVING THE "RIGHT PEOPLE" IS ONLY PART OF IT

Standards state goals, but they do not themselves provide the means or authority to change the way things are done. Teachers and principals should be held accountable to what they can control, but it is wrong and unproductive to hold them accountable when they lack the authority to change things in pursuit of their goals.

Starting with the right people does not guarantee effective schools. Altruism and passion cannot stand up to the pressures of dynamics created by poorly designed systems. Good people get rolled over by the dysfunctional incentives that allow complacency, do not reward efforts above and beyond the minimum, and fail to motivate either the students or the teachers.

Any attempts to improve schools and learning will need to work at setting the right conditions where improvement may occur.

Prevention

Redesign Schools to Improve the Lot of Those Inside Them

Arrange school to treat students as adults and teachers as professionals, preventing a whole range of maladies and inefficiencies that bleed school performance. If personal and professional integrity is encouraged, the climate for students and teachers will improve. We might be surprised how their motivation, and in turn the performance of the school, increases.

No. But show them the way to independence

Chapter Six

Understanding New Technologies in Education

School technology can be understood as the combination of labor and capital. Computers, iPads, and electronic smart boards are capital. Chalkboards, desks, books, and notebooks are capital. Teachers and students provide the labor, fitting it within a pedagogical model.

This distinction helps in the conceptualization of both sides of the equation—the labor side and the IT side—instead of limiting scope only to improving teaching or purchasing electronics.

Fundamental changes in the technology of school and education are very rare. The organization of the university brought scholars and pupils and apprentices together. The advent of the printing press was major. So was creation of the factory school. Now it is electronic technologies. K–12 has not figured this one out. (See figure 6.1.)

Instead of responding to a changing world, the institution is resisting. It does not want to change form as would be necessary. Now schools are starting to be dragged into changing, as students are using electronics whether officials forbid them or not.

There is no way to stop what is happening. Entrepreneurs are moving, quickly. Alternative options are available and accredited. The change is under way. The question facing public schooling is not if the shift will occur, but whether it will take part.

New technologies, met with fanfare and promises, regularly fail to meet or even approach their potential. A main reason why most electronics fail

Technology = Labor (teachers, students) + Capital (electronic, physical)

Figure 6.1. The components of technology

to have a significant impact on student learning is that they are used in support of existing processes. They are taken and added on to existing schools. But the factory school is not their realm. For schools to integrate electronics, they need new business models.

K–12 education is the only information industry in which the addition of advanced electronics has been cost-increasing, not cost-decreasing. In a time of strained budgets, electronics are liabilities unless they increase productivity.

THE NATURE OF LEARNING HAS MOVED FROM MASS PRODUCTION TO MASS CUSTOMIZATION

Over the past two decades the information technology revolution has transformed American industry, leading to new types of work processes and business organizations, and increasing productivity and consumer innovations.

IT has the power to dramatically remake American schooling, too. New school models enabled by IT are resulting in the emergence of mass customization—a new kind of pedagogy that is focused on meeting the needs of individual students. This marks a departure from the current pedagogy of mass production, in which all students are treated alike.

Using IT to personalize learning enables and empowers young people to pursue their own knowledge. This application of capital—the use of IT to remake learning—can be described as type 2.0. Type 2.0 learning puts the student at the center of the process by emphasizing active participation by learners, who control the pace of instruction and construct knowledge themselves. The Institute for Defense Analysis has a term for it: technology-mediated learning.

Type 2.0 learning harnesses technology in ways that inspire students to learn and conduct their own inquiries outside of the framework of traditional classes and standardized tests. The key contribution of IT is to allow a student's interests, needs, strengths, and weaknesses to drive the learning process, with the instructor facilitating rather than dictating. It allows materials to be designed much more around the needs of individual students.

IT can reengineer the "production process" of school by placing students at the center of activity. This stands in contrast to the teaching-centered pedagogy in which the teacher controls information. What is needed now is pedagogical applications of hardware and software that maximize the ability of young people to control information technology and to use it creatively. This calls for a new paradigm of student learning, overseen and assisted by teachers. With this approach, students are empowered to vary the pace at which they learn—more slowly if necessary, more rapidly if possible—and to vary what they learn.

Teachers benefit, too. This approach can produce a form of school that upgrades teachers' work from presenting material to planning, advising, and evaluating. Under this production model, not only do young people assume a greater share of labor, but the entire operation of the classroom is fundamentally altered. It is not sufficient for students to sit passively in desks while the teacher works to impart knowledge. Young people must be less restricted, less regulated—yet guided.

By redesigning school to incorporate new technologies, we can dramatically increase the personalization of education with little marginal increase in labor costs. The prospects of this change are revolutionary for an industry that spends upwards of 80 percent of its funds on personnel. Hiring twice as many teachers is prohibitively expensive, but the right application of new technologies may achieve a similar result.

THE TECHNOLOGY HAS FLIPPED FROM TEACHING-CENTERED TO LEARNING-CENTERED

The old technology of schooling sees information as scarce. Its mode is teacher-lecture, where students sit as a captive audience at desks while the teacher delivers information. Whether or not students choose to learn is up to them. Students have almost no control over content, pace, or style. Schools are fixed and ubiquitous, for purely practical reasons—what had at one time been necessary physical constraints. Choice among these options means we now do a lot of busing.

The new technology of schooling uses advancements in IT to enable new ways of organizing teachers and students. It gets at both sides of the technology equation. When both the labor and the capital are re-thought, models of school and learning may then be created that flip the dynamic—premising school on the pursuit of information by the student, instead of the pushing of information by teachers.

Customization is achieved by tailoring the pace and content of learning to an individual student's aptitudes and interests. Substance is guided through content standards, and quality is ensured by the teacher, as an adviser.

The new technology of education is a paradigm shift. Schools have not made gains because their leaders, despite good intentions, have merely crammed new electronics into existing structures. They have worked on only one side of the equation. To help clarify, each part will be taken now, separately: labor, and electronic and physical capital.

THE FIRST SIDE OF THE EQUATION: THE STRUCTURE OF LABOR

The structures exist now—and have for some time—to allow for IT innovations to make inroads and take root in schools. There is a growing national movement around this idea of radically new organization and pedagogies. Teachers are getting involved in school design. Families are demanding new ideas, and business and policy leaders are joining in.

The center of gravity is shifting from teacher-lecture to student-direction. It is difficult to resist the incessant tug toward the natural order of things. And in the United States at the end of this century's first decade, the natural order of things is resembling more and more a user-empowered, self-directed style. This has been its path since the 1980s and is growing faster by the day. The best course for architects of the public education system is to accept this and work with it.

As new models of school arise, the physical arrangement of schools will change, too. Some schools now have few walls, opting instead for common areas where students exchange their fun-size desks for real adult workstations.

It is possible to change the management model of schools and districts, including giving teachers and principals greater decision-making authority. The teacher-partnership arrangement, in which teachers run a school through committees and elected leaders, is among the most innovative. Project-based learning, hybrid online/bricks-and-mortar, and electronic intelligent tutoring are some of the alternative pedagogies.

The development of alternative labor models is improving the uptake of new electronics. Teachers and principals are assuming greater degrees of decision-making authority and applying electronics as they see fit. School designs and pedagogies are also emerging that break from the factory schools' constraints and allow students and teachers to explore how best to use IT.

THE SECOND SIDE OF THE EQUATION: ELECTRONIC AND PHYSICAL CAPITAL

The cloud is the driver here. (Cloud computing is an Internet-based, shared-resource process.) Documents, applications, and learning systems will continue to go up onto it. As the story goes, Bill Gates once said that at the outset of Microsoft he never suspected computers would become simply "dumb" portals to the Internet.

Not only has that happened, it has also thrown open the accessibility of top-shelf technologies. If each computer had to hold its own applications for Facebook, Wikipedia, and e-mail, their cost would be prohibitive. But these things are hosted now on the Internet. Encyclopedias used to be computer based; now they are on the cloud. E-mail used to be managed by applications stored on a hard drive. G-mail and Yahoo have taken most of that business. Soon, Microsoft Office applications will follow.

Students are not limited to PCs and laptops but can start using all available devices to access programs and information. This arrangement can adapt to any new technological advance that comes along.

Meanwhile, the need for traditional computers is decreasing. In 2009 approximately 20 percent of iPhone purchases were by people who had never owned a computer—both young people and lower-income folks who were already buying iPods. In 2010 the iPad followed. The laptop industry is undergoing a disruptive change as well.

The common consumer instruments will continue to become more advanced. First the phone was ubiquitous; then the MP3 player as a second device; then the phone and a camera together; then the phone, camera, and MP3 player all in one. The Internet came into handheld form from business-only specialty devices to the common consumer all in one. This trend will continue.

Most people do not need a sit-down word processor, so cloud-based documents will be sufficient. Remember: IT is not static. This book went to press in 2011. In 2013 readers will be surrounded by a new range of devices with new capabilities. The dual-touch technology created by Apple will migrate from the iPhone and iPad into wider uses.

By 2015 personal computing and handhelds will have changed significantly. By 2020, the technologies of 2011 will have undergone a qualitative shift. If the arrangements of technology-mediated learning are set right, additional innovations may be adopted and applied as they are picked up in society.

THERE IS A GROWING DISCONNECT BETWEEN STUDENTS AND TEACHERS

Prohibition of electronics is unrealistic. The factory school runs against human nature in predictable ways. Young adults today expect open access to information as a matter of course. They use electronics fluidly in their lives and expect the same at school.

Young people and adults have very different understandings of modern technology. There is a significant and growing disconnect between how students and their teachers view the role, importance, and progress of electronics and the Internet in the classroom. Despite their ubiquitous nature in today's society, most adult educators—even recent college graduates—are failing to grasp the implications of the past 10 years' technological gains on the lives of young people.

The evidence is compelling that teachers and administrators are not on the same page as younger people, according to a series of national surveys:[25]

- While almost 50 percent of educators think that students learn about technology in school, only 15 percent of those in grades 6–12 agree. The vast majority say they learn it from friends, or on their own.
- Among those middle and high school students who believe that their technology skills are advanced, only 23 percent feel their school is doing a good job preparing them for the work world.
- Student access to mobile devices has been increasing rapidly. From 2006–2007, the use of MP3 players by K–2 students was 84 percent, with 58 percent for those in grades 3–5. The number of middle and high

school students with smart phones increased by more than 44 percent. More than 50 percent of middle and high school students want to use these mobile devices to work on school projects and to communicate with classmates.

Students are interested in increasing their productivity through online tools and downloading information. These technologies are so new and advancing so quickly—44 percent growth in smart phones over just one year at 2010—that pedagogy is simply not keeping up. While word processors influenced the workings of education from 1990 to 2000, these devices are having an exponentially more disruptive effect for the classes of 2010 and later. The revolution is under way outside the classroom, and is beginning to breach the school walls. Three distinct trends are becoming increasingly clear:

1. Young people are agitated by restrictions on their usage of technologies in school: Internet filters, limits on computer access, and prohibitions against cell phones, iPods, iPads, and so on.
2. Young people feel a sense of entitlement over technology and their devices. Students want authority to use the same gadgets in school that they use at home and have them with them when they walk in the school doors.
3. There is a growing gap between student and adult perceptions of technology in education—of its present and future roles, of its importance. The disconnect is pronounced already between today's high schoolers and young adults just 10 years older.

Young people want to use their tech devices, and they expect autonomy. Even new teachers are finding themselves entering an entirely new youth culture. New college graduates are natives to the digital age, but they cannot integrate new electronics into a closed and inflexible model.

In addition to looking within the schools for new applications of technology, we should be looking in part to the outside: to new entrants to the teaching profession, to the gaming industry, to software developers, and to entrepreneurs generally.

Utilization

Get Creative with Staffing

Supplement the professional teachers with differentiated staffing. At present, schools employ aides for special education, libraries, and technology. There are other ways, too:

- Fully incorporate student teachers and young service volunteers.
- Contract with IT firms to integrate new technology models. The School of One in New York runs a very promising IT-based model made possible by its partnership with the for-profit Wireless Generation.
- Expand the role of students as peer teachers.
- Use associate teachers to lengthen the school day, with some starting earlier and some staying later to work with students individually before and after classes.
- One inner-city high school hired a young graduate as a social, disciplinary, and academic ombudsman. By floating the school and classrooms he seeks and irons out social wrinkles before they become gang problems, and he mentors students. It is a significant relief for the teachers.
- Bring on retirees as teaching coaches, aides, mentors, and support staff.

Chapter Seven

Properly Applying Information Technologies in Education

When traders monitor security markets, they sometimes look for the introduction of new technologies to a company. Analysts work to identify when a firm has found new ways to combine capital and human labor: a revised process of production, a reorganization of management, or improved mechanisms for distribution. Innovations in capital and labor can lead to dramatic improvements in the efficiency and effectiveness of an operation.

Then there is the combination of these new technologies with innovations in business models. Henry Ford's assembly line led to economies of scale, and just-in-time manufacturing from Japan offsets a lack of space for warehousing. Today, business models that thrive on decentralized design and production and strip goods to bare essentials make a sort of "frugal innovation" that is stemming from emerging markets and threatening to disrupt the markets in the developed world.

British economist Peter Stanyer has a set of basic questions that he asks when assessing the introduction of new technologies into a company:[26]

- Does the technology represent only a one-time blip in the company's performance?
- Does it represent a step-change in the firm's future profits?
- Will it result in a sustained increased growth rate?

In these cases new technology, if it is successful, is understood to increase productivity.

Three enduring motifs:
Accessing, processing, and communicating information.

Figure 7.1. The motifs of technological progress

THE MARCH OF IT IS CLEAR

It is important to understand that we are still in the early stages of information technologies. Paper has been around for thousands of years, and the printing press for hundreds. The information technologies of the 21st century are unlike anything our society has ever seen. They are advancing at an unrelenting pace toward a few enduring motifs: the ability to access information, to process it into knowledge, and to present it and communicate it.

In the early stages information technology was basic—word processing, spreadsheets. After some time they evolved to begin mimicking human processes, such as simple read/test programs in early online education, instead of lecture/test in a classroom. The technology has now moved ahead, one full stage further.

Ted Kolderie has observed that "our discussion about digital electronics has not yet really begun to think about the Web as a whole world for young people to explore, in which they can see things and get information and do research . . . and in which they can do this individually."[27]

The situation is made more interesting in that we can see the wave of technology coming, even as we experience its swelling. The technology available today will only be better tomorrow, and those beyond are different from what we can image today. Kolderie has sketched out some evidence that the capacity of technology continues to march on:

- Moore's Law continues to hold. The computing power of a chip has doubled every 18 months for 40 years.
- The price of processing power has fallen steadily: $480 per MIPS (million instructions per second) for the Intel 086 in 1978, $50 per MIPS for the Intel 386 in 1985, $4 per MIPS for the Pentium Pro in 1995, $2 per MIPS for the Itanium 2 in 2003, and pennies per MIPS in 2010.
- Hard drive storage capacity has doubled every 19 months, and the cost of a stored megabyte of data has fallen 50 percent per year. The cost of

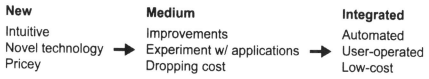

New	Medium	Integrated
Intuitive	Improvements	Automated
Novel technology ➤	Experiment w/ applications ➤	User-operated
Pricey	Dropping cost	Low-cost

Figure 7.2.   Refinement of technology

storing one megabyte of information fell, too: It was $5,257 in 1975, 17 cents in 1999, half a cent in 2002, and a minute fraction of that in 2010.
* There were 182 million websites at the beginning of 2009, and that number had doubled from two years prior.
* All of this permits companies to put terabytes into pocket drives, and for Google to provide over 7 gigabytes of storage for a user of Gmail's free service. By the time this book goes to print, these capacities will have increased 20–30 percent.

New software will look more tutorial than it will look like the traditional courseware that supports the teacher-led process. "At the heart of this evolution is the conversion of complex, intuitive processes into simple, rules-based work." A handoff, Christensen says, from hiring more expensive, highly trained teachers to incorporating electronics instead.

As new electronics move from the cutting edge to mainstream, their cost drops. The product becomes refined and is built upon, and users discover more applications for it. If paired with an organizational model that can properly apply them, electronics can become more accessible, effective, and affordable all at once.

Merely adding electronics to the teacher-lecture model would be like using fuel cells to make magazine delivery trucks more efficient, while competitors move their content online for instant, customized delivery. One approach uses new technology to support the existing process, the other to remake it.

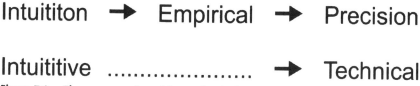

Intuititon ➤ Empirical ➤ Precision

Intuititive .... ➤ Technical

Figure 7.3.   The progress of precision technologies

DISINTERMEDIATION

Developments in technology tend to downplay or do away with the need for intermediaries. The telephone industry found improved productivity through a change from manual to electronic switchboards. Airlines allow passengers to print boarding passes at kiosks. An entire generation is coming of age having hardly ever encountered a bank teller, thanks to the advent of ATMs.

In each of these cases economic and operational efficiencies were found through a disintermediation that reduced the costs of labor by substituting new technologies.

The process of disintermediation is at work in finance, shifting savings from institutional banks to money markets. It has led to an explosion in personal investment management, with people exercising control over their own portfolios. The volume of trading in security markets has grown exponentially over the past two decades, now that trading can be done electronically, off the trading floor.

Some are quick to argue that education is different—that no serious productivity increases through disintermediation are possible because it is labor dependent. This is unlikely. Opportunities for improving productivity are always opening, as technology is constantly improving and the world is evolving.

Take, for example, the U.S. Postal Service. The system is world class. Standard mail can go from California to New York in a couple of days, reliably. Or from Chicago to London in half a week. The Postal Service uses cars, trucks, trains, and planes to run an efficient system of distribution. The introduction of automation in the sorting and management of logistics was a huge jump. How could this possibly be significantly improved upon? Through disintermediation, or cutting out physical distribution lines. In 1990 few could see the coming impact of e-mail.

Or consider a professional symphony, certainly one of the less elastic groupings of workers in terms of improving efficiency. The musicians practice independently, so as to make the most of their time together with the conductor. When they play, the members perform with great skill and professionalism. So how could the symphony be made more productive with little marginal increase of labor? The musicians cannot simply play more quickly, or more loudly (though they could be amplified, or they could play in a larger venue over many nights to reach more people).

When phonograph recording first came into the marketplace, accessibility to large ensembles opened wide up. Much more music was produced, with little if any additional expenditure from the musicians. The great standing orchestras of the 20th century—in New York, in Vienna—were not going to travel from town to town performing in living rooms, so they recorded themselves playing and licensed it. The phonograph was a productivity gain for symphonies and string ensembles.

Discovery by trial is the only sure road ahead at this early point. Entrepreneurs are flying at full speed developing useful applications of new technologies that will improve productivity and value. While searching for one sort of new technology application in schooling, we may well stumble on something that is at present completely unknown.

VARIABLE DISINTERMEDIATION:
TECHNOLOGY-MEDIATED LEARNING

The future of electronic learning is going to be much more sophisticated than the image many people have of a young person sitting in the basement alone, clicking away for hours—this binary frame of reading screens versus listening in a classroom.

Nor is it quite right to talk about all forms of electronic learning as "online." This term too is dated and probably will not stay around. Instead something like "virtual" better encompasses that which happens outside of the physical realm, and "e-learning" is being used to describe the growing use of electronics and software in the education process.

One promising model, which both more closely resembles real-world work and is often more intrinsically interesting to students, is project-based learning. The focus in project-based learning is on letting students learn in areas that interest them, guided by content requirements, rather than on teaching every child the exact same information.

The resources available today for project-based learning are considerable and are developing rapidly, as Web-based information grows and as search engines help support it. Broadband networks make it possible for students to team up with others, including professionals, elsewhere. Handheld mobile devices make it possible both to study lessons and to communicate with partners and teachers from remote, off-site locations. Intelligent tutoring software is taking an intuitive practice and automating it.

A leading example of project-based learning is Minnesota's New Country School, located in the rural town of Henderson in southern Minnesota. New Country School is a teacher-run cooperative chartered school with a project-based pedagogy. Each student has a personal workstation, complete with a desk and a personal computer.

Students work with advisers to meet course content requirements. They can incorporate IT in any way they see helpful: e-mail, podcasts, online specialty courses, personalized tutoring software. Web-based document programs allow teachers to jointly review work. The school describes itself as follows:

> The school is based upon the idea that students will be most engaged in the learning process when they have a personal interest in what they are learning. Instead of sitting in a teacher-driven classroom all day long, students learn through the exploration of topics that interest them on their own terms, and largely at their own pace. Each student is a member of a team of twelve to twenty students, managed by an adult advisor who helps to facilitate the learning process. Instead of grades, students receive credit for their work. The process is completely flexible, and can be tailored toward specific learning styles, prior student knowledge, student motivation, etc.

School of One, a start-up in New York City's public school system, has found a way to flip the learning dynamic to student driven, with a new classroom model and a new computer program.

The professionals at School of One—some of whom are contracted business partners who assist the teachers—take information from students, including their interests and skills, and work them into a computer program that tailors the character and content of lessons. Students get captured by the work, quickly.

While eight elementary students work intently on a math program, five others work in a group and seven are gathered in the corner with the teacher receiving a tutorial. Not only does the atmosphere improve, but the teachers will tell you that the net labor at work in the room is many times that of the traditional program.

Entering the classroom, with walls knocked down and computer pods throughout, the observer is struck by how much more it feels like Google's offices than a school—and by how quiet it is. Everyone is working. Perhaps most interesting to the observer, it just feels right. The learning model is multimodal, and technology-mediated learning is strikingly effective at pinpointing and revisiting students' individual deficiencies. It is a design of the future, combining a new school model with new uses for technology.

Another model is the School of the Future in Philadelphia, which is instructive both for its successes and its struggles. In a public/private partnership, Microsoft Corporation teamed with Philadelphia public schools to design a school that, while within the district's budget, could make IT ubiquitous. They added smart boards, laptops, and keyless entry.

By 2009 it was becoming apparent that the school could not maintain its culture or cost structure. Nor was it particularly more effective. The designers of this school made the same mistake that so many others have made in bringing electronics into schools, merely adding them onto the existing business model, adding financial and practical liability without also changing the arrangement or the labor model of the school. (See figure 7.4.)

New electronics are useless unless paired with the right organizational model and school culture. And many times the tail of their operational costs is not accounted for. The electronics are bought, but costs associated with its maintenance and training are left to later decision. If neither an organizational model or a culture were put in place ahead of time, the likelihood is low that the electronics end up saving money or improving productivity.

For students to maximize IT for learning, they need freedom of movement. They will use e-mail, computers, and social networking on their own. Schools should harness this reality and design incentives to get students to direct their energies. Lay out a process for helping them understand what needs to be done, for example—then judge on deliverables. Let them decide how particular technologies will or will not help.

Electronics should be cost decreasing, not cost increasing. Right now new technologies are stuck in unmalleable, high-cost institutions.

$$\text{Disruptive Innovation} = \text{Technological Innovation} + \text{Business Model Innovation}$$

Figure 7.4.   Disruptive technologies

As electronics are added to the factory school they add cost, without achieving a significant increase in productivity. The result is a decreased value of school. The increase in *productivity* occurs when IT is used to increase the labor of students, while optimizing the work of teachers. The same number of paid staff is on hand, but output rises.

The real reduction in *costs* happen when schools move away from the expensive and inefficient factory model and get into alternative designs that require less money to operate. The contribution of IT is in enabling this change, increasing the value of schools by improving the cost/performance proposition.

THE PACE OF THE UPTAKE OF NEW TECHNOLOGIES IS DECEPTIVE IN ITS EARLY STAGES

It is easy to write off the early years of a new technology, while it is still in its development stages. A 30 percent annual growth rate in the first five years looks deceptively tame.

Online learning in post-secondary education was not taken seriously through the 1990s and was treated with skepticism during the 2000s. But it maintained a dramatic growth trajectory—most observers just did not see it or did not want to see it. The growth of chartering in many urban areas looks modest from a one- or even three-year perspective, but 20 years out a 15-percent net annual increase in enrollment looks pretty dramatic.

Clayton Christensen, Curt Johnson, and Michael Horn now argue convincingly that computer-based learning will make up half of the "seat-miles" in K–12 by 2020.[28] They contend that this country is leaving the early stages in an S-curve of technology's incorporation into K–12. Starting slow, with token inclusion of new devices or software—computers the past 20 years, smart boards today—a period of experimentation has been under way. As useful new innovations in electronics alternative school models are developed, a sharp increase will begin as they are adopted as a best practice. Their model predicts that this steep trajectory will hold for a time, before leveling off after the innovation has had sufficient time to be absorbed by the marketplace.

This is the trajectory followed by other disruptive innovations through history, such as the replacement of the horse and buggy by the car, the tube-powered radio by solid-state transistors, and the typewriter by the

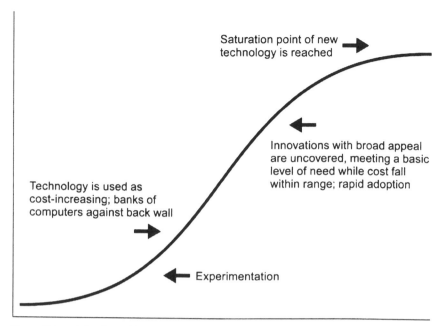

Figure 7.5. Adoption of breakthrough technologies in education (S-curve)

computer. In each case the disruptive innovations, while slow to begin, were rapid in their uptake once the right combination of cost, benefit, and effectiveness was struck.

It will take time at first for a culture to build. The supply and the market for IT—self-directed learning, intelligent tutoring, real-time assessments—have previously been limited, and so the culture is yet to be established.

Many students and teachers will not want or need to use a new technology at its outset. That is fine. For some, especially in traditional schools, electronics will not represent an immediate gain in appeal, efficiency, or effectiveness. But as the technology advances, effectiveness goes up, cost goes down, and appeal widens.

As technologies advance, intelligent tutoring programs will move closer and closer to matching one-on-one personal interaction. They could, in fact, surpass the effectiveness of humans. Systems used in training by the Department of Defense have been shown already to improve student performance by approximately one standard deviation—a move by a student, for example, from the 60th percentile among his or her peers to the 85th or 90th.

This envisions a partial move from teaching-as-art to teaching-by-engineering. As computer-aided learning become increasingly sophisticated, the technologies will present unprecedented capabilities for the empirical study of learning and real-time feedback. Alterations, additions, and supplements to the learning process could be performed with scientific precision—a game-changing proposition.

Substitution and Optimization

Tap into Unpaid Labor with Technology-Mediated Learning

Substitute student labor for the hiring of additional teachers, and optimize the role of those already on staff. Technology-mediated learning driven by student efforts can lead to a qualitative leap in productivity for the same cost of labor. The number of teachers remains constant, but the nature of their work moves from presenting information to guiding and shaping (students self-access instead). This will improve retention, and if combined with expanding the professional roles of teachers may attract higher-caliber people into the profession.

This is a self-help model for students, giving them the tools and having them provide the labor. Done right, the net level of labor in a classroom can go up 10 or 15 times.

Part Four

MOVING THE STRATEGY FORWARD

The goal of local, state, and federal policy should be to create a sound system of schooling inside the public sector. Dynamism, openness and competition, and light but effective regulations are some of the characteristics of a well-functioning public education system.

The split-screen strategy is a third way for improvement, moving beyond the efforts of exhortation and punishment on the one side, and subsidy and protection on the other.

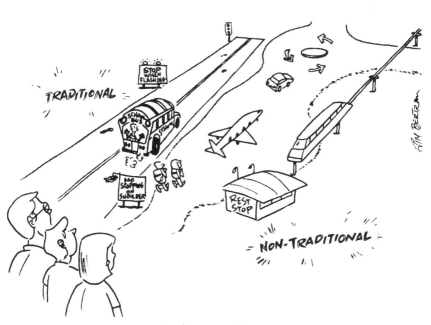

A split-screen strategy.

But it is not enough to "create the capacity for change." That is the first step, as Ted Kolderie says. This country needs now a redoubled effort at innovation in forms of school, finding ways to capture and channel disruptive technologies to radically remake the learning process.

Public policy can help this process by removing barriers and actively changing the character of the system. The goal is to create a system that encourages innovation and can cultivate and manage plurality.

The government should continue to move from being the sole provider of education to its buyer and regulator, contracting with public and private nonprofit and for-profit organizations to provide desired services. This greatly expands the options available to public leadership and opens the doors to a virtually limitless supply of talent and energy.

State legislatures and related education authorities should first move to clear away any obstacles to change, then divide regulation and oversight into two entities: one suited for the traditional management of schools and the other for an innovative sector of the system.

At the district level, following the lead of some of the nation's largest cities, the leaders of school districts should run their own internal split-screens, setting up innovation sectors with their own executive team reporting directly to the board. The role of the district board then evolves from administering a single model of schools to managing a portfolio of school providers and models.

At the federal level, the president and Congress can help ease the process for innovation by expanding the No Child Left Behind Act to include a broader understanding of what counts as achievement in learning. The federal government can also provide seed money to create state-level innovation entities and use them as vehicles for federal grants.

Perhaps the most significant tool Washington has is the president's authority to speak directly to state legislatures and help set the agenda. This strategy was shown to be effective during the Race to the Top program in 2009–2010, and it could direct the federal desire to be involved in public schooling away from regulation and toward system improvement.

Chapter Eight

Policy Opportunities

One difference between this book's critique of things and the criticism of others is that it sees poor performance not fundamentally as a problem of the people in public education, but of the design of the system in which they operate. Any real or perceived problems of student motivation, teacher quality, stubbornness of teacher unions, ineffective leadership, or the untenable cost structure of K–12 can all be addressed by changing the character and the incentives of the system.

Frontal conflict is the vogue. It is easy. But it targets behaviors instead of getting to the cause of those behaviors. In an interdependent system where dynamics trump altruism and incentives drive actions, frontal conflict as anything more than a selective tool is not only ineffective, but lazy and strategically unwise.

This chapter will provide a model, derived from discussions in Minnesota and large school districts across the country, to help facilitate openness, competition, and innovation—all inside the public system.

Effective reform need not be sweeping or comprehensive to be consequential. Go upstream. Significant changes can be realized by seemingly small alterations to the fabric of the system. The mechanism of chartering schools was not appreciated at first for its potential to reshape the schooling landscape. Nor is it fully appreciated now, still in the early stages of manifestation.

The Site-Governed Schools (SGS) law in Minnesota and the related Innovation Schools law of 2010 in Massachusetts have similar potential. These reforms are changes to the framework of educational systems. They open up opportunity in the system for people to create new, different public schools in a unionized setting.

With frustration about the performance of schools being so strong and the cost pressures being so serious, there is a lot of pressure built up that can take advantage of just these opportunities.

KEEP REGULATION LIGHT AND SMART

There are two basic approaches to regulating schools: direct control, and facilitation and oversight. A rigid, centralized organization locks a system into linear movements. Fluidity and segmentation, on the other hand, open the capacity for variability and innovation, which drive improvement.

The strategy behind vouchers is to break away from command and control. The voucher strategy allows for maximum student choice but runs into trouble on questions of quality control, accountability, and coherency. The public has shown, rightly or wrongly, that it just will not accept vouchers as a systemwide strategy. Vouchers are a tool.

Yet continuing with the command-and-control district/agency model is not possible if we seek a more innovative, responsive, and accountable system.

Both the market approach and command and control have a role in such a large and important public good as public schooling. It is possible to combine them into a sound market system.

Command-and-control regulation is vulnerable to failure and inefficiency. It is fraught with perverse incentives, minimizes teacher and student motivation, and—as is the nature of centralized power—invites corruption.

The benefit to a decentralized strategy by a district or state is that the basic incentives for efficiency, responsiveness, and continual improvement can be built in. In this sort of arrangement, the proper functions of district boards and state authorities are quite different than direct management. Instead, their role is the rule setting and oversight. There is a practical element, too. Command-and-control management requires continual policing by an authority, while facilitation and oversight does not.

Regulatory design affects a system's capacity to handle plurality. By decentralizing school control, an education system can be more responsive to the many different needs, tastes, and abilities of its students and teachers. The regulatory style of facilitation and oversight enables the emergence of market forces—identifying and responding to student

↳ *This is based on #!*

needs, encouraging entrepreneurship, rewarding the best through increased enrollment—inside a publicly funded and regulated system.

The character of a legal and regulatory system plays out in the incentives it creates. As authority is decentralized, those given more responsibility must be under sufficient incentive to make the right decisions for the public good. Smart regulation does not try to prescribe the desired behavior of people in the system (the present strategy) but establishes the conditions that will produce the behavior at a high and reliable frequency through individuals' free will.

To improve schools some sort of decentralized regulatory framework is needed. To get extraordinary performance, schools cannot be uniform. While schools are compelled by law to provide an equal education, nowhere does it say they must be identical.

The present system contains a regulatory bias that privileges traditional schools over alternative models. Established interests are present and well represented, and have an ability to limit innovation when it would unbalance their position. They can exclude the new and different through use of entry controls such as caps on chartering, limits on the kinds of people who are allowed to start new schools or teach in them, or making the process to gain the necessary independence for an innovative school impossible or onerous.

Innovation creates uncertainty. In the present system, school boards, state agencies, and political leaders have incentive to not upset the balance in an environment where interests and resources are interdependent. The players sign up for the easy strategy of growth, without doing things differently. They build and dismantle empires—they do not design for change. Focus is on growing resources, the number and qualification of teachers, the level and evaluation of standards. It is the convenient approach, but it is not the right one.

The demand for alternatives is already present, and there is certainly further latent demand for new types of school. We will not fully know what demands are there until a more thorough supply is created. Demand for different choices will grow as people discover there are alternatives available. People cannot choose what does not exist. It is difficult to imagine the alternatives without knowing what else might be.

Because of the need to identify new alternatives, it is not good enough to work only with what has been "proven to work." Everything good today was at one point new and unproven. The emergence of new types of schools and new applications of IT is not precisely predictable. In the beginning of an innovation, the trailblazers do not know for certain how it will turn out. They suspect, anticipate, plan. They operate from an informed intuition and whatever applicable research exists.

But if something is truly new there will be risk. A strategy of innovation requires a regulatory arrangement that can tolerate risk. The body that regulates risktakers must have an appreciation and tolerance for risk. And as long as students have the choice to attend or not attend, policy can and should tolerate some uncertainty for the prospect of gain.

STATE-LEVEL ACTIONS

The responsibility for public education rests with the states. Washington leverages money to gain influence, but state legislators are the architects of the system. Here is where the most consequential changes can be made.

State education agencies have gotten good at managing the existing system. They have helped build it out and have served it effectively. Their staffs are skilled, well intentioned, and competent. But the agencies are not designed to run an innovation scheme of any significant size or scope.

For that we need to move one step higher, to the state legislatures. Legislators should make it easier for districts to create schools with autonomy and exemptions from regulation reflective of chartering, to allow district boards to establish schools that report directly to them. The Minnesota legislature took this step first in 2009. Massachusetts moved in the same direction in 2010. Many of the major urban districts in the country have been working on this for some time now, as part of efforts to innovate and evolve.

Policymakers should also establish infrastructure to provide leadership and support for the creation of many different kinds of schools. They may set up a state-level, legislatively authorized nonprofit organization and charge it with fostering innovation and providing technical assistance to school entrepreneurs. They can make it responsible for identifying the most qualified authorizers of new schools and for managing federal and other funds to facilitate planning and start-ups.

A possible model for this is shown in figure 8.1. In this arrangement the existing state agency is responsible for overseeing the traditional schools in both the districts and chartered schools. Meanwhile, a new entity oversees the nontraditional, innovative schools, which exist both inside districts and in the chartering sector.

Splitting the function into two bodies takes innovation out from under the control of the conventional and protects the start-ups from the inertia of established cultures and processes. The goal here is to separate the regulatory body responsible for the disruptive, paradigm-shifting innovations from the regulatory body that was designed to manage the traditional schools—two different regulatory models for two different strategies, each with its own characteristics and incentives.

It is also important to separate oversight from technical assistance. These are two different functions. The state has ultimate oversight, but a separate entity can do the development work. This arrangement is more likely to facilitate progress without unnecessary levels of controls.

The state-level entity on the innovation side could be run as a nongovernmental body with a board appointed by the governor and by legislative leadership. The schools it works with would be new, independent, and innovative. They would be overseen by government-approved authorizers, as chartered schools are in most states.

The tasks of the body in both the charter and district sectors include leveraging political, human, and financial resources; providing leadership and help generating financial and other support for innovative schools; approving chartered school sponsors; and directing alternative assessment and research programs that better suit an R & D operation.

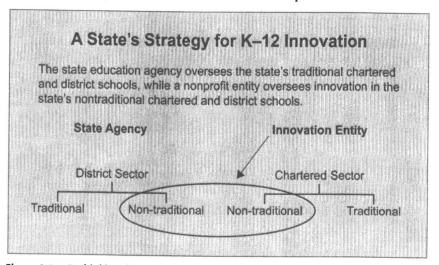

Figure 8.1.   Rethinking the state regulatory system

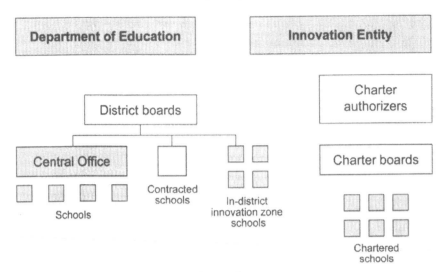

Figure 8.2.   The framework of a well-designed system

This model could have real power: to facilitate public grants and raise private resources, to set and remove binding regulations, and to execute legislative or gubernatorial directives. This innovation entity would assume from the state agency tasks of R & D that are better suited for an independent body.

Its purpose would be to see that the process of innovation happens. The organization would not implement innovations—that is the role of teachers and education entrepreneurs. It may house funds to aid replication of effective models, but replication is not its main function. Instead, its role is to foster entrepreneurship, encourage reimagining of business models, and clear the way of any undue hindrances or roadblocks.

Governors should take the lead in these reforms, bringing plans to the legislature. Governors have both a convening power and a unique ability to set the policy agenda of a state. Where the governor does not act, the legislature can.

DISTRICT-LEVEL ACTIONS

Following the lead of some of the nation's largest cities, the top policy-making bodies of school districts (the board or mayor) should run their own internal split screens, setting up innovation sectors with their own executive team reporting directly to the board. The role of the district board evolves from administering a single model of schools to managing a portfolio of school providers and models.

The schools should be independent and responsible to deliver on individually negotiated performance contracts. Exempt them from compliance with district policies, and strike a deal with unions so teachers may elect to forego contract restrictions.

The factory school is in its most dire financial condition in rural areas with declining populations. Enduring round after round of painful consolidations, rural districts now need to look to new forms of school as a matter of survival.

When the factory model is assumed as the only way to organize learning, district leaders believe it is appropriate to do whatever is necessary to reach an economy of scale. Yet the very notion of economy of scale has been turned upside down. The options for rural districts now are no longer limited to cutting services or expanding boundaries. Electronic learning offers ways to meet the low-volume and specialized needs of these schools, because "scale" is shared by users of a program, globally. Learning models that recognize and apply this new reality can fill out the offerings of rural schools and help keep them rooted locally.

School districts should move quickly now at innovating to find new and better ways of doing things. A large part of this will include the creation of new schools that are based on more cost-viable organizational models and innovate in their use of new technologies.

Many districts are creating innovation zones that go a significant distance in creating the conditions for R & D. It varies by city. The New York Department of Education is pushing authority out into the schools in a "systemic dismantling of the system as we know it," a senior administration put it.

Boston has been running the pilot schools system for almost two decades now, as a competitive response to chartering.

Los Angeles has decided to try to remake its schools through a large, decentralized contracting scheme that will grant control of up to a quarter of the schools to the most creative and competent bidders.

Except for those districts under mayoral control, school boards are the policymaking body and the superintendent works for them. The best setup for an innovation sector sets it outside of the traditional realm, with its own executive who reports to the board. The model of Dayton-Hudson and Target, described in chapter 1, provides the archetype here. No city does this at present, relying instead on the direction of an administrator who reports to the superintendent for changes. That can work, but it is more volatile.

Districts can apply emerging technologies such as online learning or intelligent tutoring to new school models, or they can use communication tools to teach one course to multiple locations at the same time. They can break up inefficient factory schools and create models of schools that are sustainable at a smaller scale. They can give teachers room to run the schools themselves. Let them make decisions. Districts do not need to link every administrative task, content standard, or rule of practice to the central office. It presents a conflict to put those responsible for running schools in charge of their oversight.

Districts should create more schools that follow the super-model paradigm, existing as independent engines of innovation that work on productivity, effectiveness, and cost daily. Districts will have to understand that they are creating competitors to their established programs. But the alternative is less appealing still—if they don't do it, someone else will.

FEDERAL-LEVEL ACTIONS

Over the past two decades, Washington has made major moves into states' operation of public education. It has done this through its constitutional authority to monitor and ensure equal rights and by linking federal money to desired regulations.

But the states are still the designers and the deciders, and state legislators are the architects of the nation's 50 different education systems. The federal government only has constitutional control over one system—the District of Columbia.

There are two particular things that can be done at the federal level. First, the president and Congress can help ease the process for innovation by expanding the No Child Left Behind Act to include a broader understanding of what counts as achievement in learning.

Second, the federal government can provide seed money to create state-level innovation entities and use them as vehicles for federal grants.

Perhaps the most significant tool Washington has is the president's authority to speak directly to state legislatures and help set the agenda. This strategy was shown to be effective during the Race to the Top program in 2009–2010, and it could direct the federal desire to be involved in K–12 away from regulation and toward system improvement.

Regulation

Create "Education Boards"

Ted Kolderie has observed that there is a basic flaw in the structure of districts: Those responsible for overseeing schools are the ones responsible for running them. Divide the oversight function from running the schools—making boards the contractors, stewards of the public interest.

Slowly, steadily, some district boards are moving away from direct management of schools and toward oversight of performance contracts with teachers and providers. This could go further: Playing the role of "education board," directors may secure schooling options for the students in a particular region without preference to particular models. This arrangement can increase accountability as the education board assumes the role of contractor and authorizer. They may organize schools by charter, employing one of the growing number of in-district autonomous school policies and laws, or through partnerships in addition to the traditional arrangement.

Understand that the board is responsible for seeing that effective education takes place, not to run schools themselves. "School boards" see themselves as administering schools. As the policy body of a district, the responsibilities of directors of an education board should be to best serve students, without preference or prejudice for particular organizational models.

Chapter Nine

Solutions to Barriers

Many of those interested in education reform have gotten themselves deeply invested in particular positions, assertions, and ideologies. By staking reputations on effects of the system, it can be difficult for otherwise well-meaning people to overcome personal interest and work on the underlying causes.

Critics also are often politically invested in conflict, and many have careers for which controversy and media coverage are their lifeblood. Others are frustrated and angry. Their emotions risk clouding judgment. For too many their entrenchment leads away from cooperating with the other side. This biases them against those solutions in which everyone wins—which are often the best ones.

But there is no need to despair. It is possible to make progress, by approaching the problems from the systemic perspective instead of getting bogged down in debates about the behavior of the professionals or particular kinds of schools.

If presented with the right strategies, people with differences are willing and able to work together. Seemingly intractable problems often do in fact have solutions if we step back and take the perspective of the system as an entity that may be changed to elicit different behavior.

Following is an attempt to lay out some common problems and offer strategies to address them based upon observations of schools, school systems, and the incentives they create.

Problem: The factory model of school is not financially viable.
Solution: Other models of school are—it is okay to change.

The large, comprehensive school is an expensive model, and the command-and-control form of regulation is inefficient. The result is a remarkably poor value for the taxpayer. Productivity is limited by the physical capacity of the teacher. And each year that costs rise without a matching increase in performance, the system becomes increasingly inefficient.

This problem can be addressed at both the school level and the system level. Across the country there are school and governance arrangements that require less funding to operate. These super-model schools (see chapter 1) are much smaller and independent, held accountable for deliverables. They are able to control functions that affect their effectiveness and cost structure, including all matters relating to school, schedule, budget, staffing, and management.

Online schools demonstrate how it is possible to improve the productivity of the adult teacher by leveraging open information sources to have the student engage and assume more of the workload.

Meanwhile, technology-mediated learning can increase productivity by enlisting student labor. Differentiating content and pace of instruction engages students, allowing them to assume a greater amount of the work of learning at no additional cost in paid labor. The application of these new technologies requires alternative business models that are more open and amenable to innovation.

Problem: Performance of students is stagnant.
Solution: Align self-interest with the public interest.

The shift from mass production to mass customization requires a change in both the technology used in schools, and their labor and organizational structure.

Until the IT revolution the school model could take on different forms, but the technology was limited. Books and paper were the tools of learning. Now that information is readily available through the Internet and accessible by electronics, entirely new forms of schooling are possible.

The future will be owned by teachers and entrepreneurs who find new ways to combine innovations in technology and innovations in business models to remake school around learning, not teaching. These schools will take different forms, many of which we have not yet seen.

If mass production was the model to fit the needs and technology of the 20th century, mass customization is the model for the 21st. As a union leader put it, "mass customization is the only true way no child will be left behind."

Problem: There is resistance to change.
Solution: Run a split-screen strategy.

Use an enabling approach to change, making it possible for people to do things differently but without compelling anyone. Many students, families, and teachers will still prefer traditional schools, and they may choose those. Others will prefer alternatives, and they should be allowed to go to those.

This country should work hard to improve its existing schools, while running a full-fledged effort at innovation in a separate R & D sector designed specially for innovation. This method avoids the resistance and unnecessary conflicts that come with forcing people to change. It also allows innovation to generate new schools organically, in response to student and teacher demands.

Innovation carries risk, but not as much risk as betting all the chips on any one reform idea. A split-screen strategy hedges that uncertainty, placing two bets at once: one on improving the traditional, and another on innovation.

Problem: K–12 is rife with the "politics of blocking."
Solution: Get actors to work through self-interest, toward the public interest.

There is a lot of conflict in the education debates, particularly about the role of unions and public administrators in blocking reform. But perhaps the right path here is less dramatic. It is the classic strategy of channeling self-interest: Make teachers the agents of change by placing them in control of their school's form and function. Increase the incentive for district leaders to innovate by removing laws and regulations that provide favored status to any particular kind of school. Give school leaders more control, and hold them accountable for deliverables.

The problem of blocking change is not exclusive to teacher unions. The administrators in state agencies and in the schools and districts are often unwilling or uninterested in doing things differently. This situation is structural. The job of a principal, superintendent, or bureaucrat is to make the existing system run as well as possible—not necessarily to change it.

The blocking of reforms may be happening because there is no obvious self-interest for those involved. Policymakers can address this with the split-screen strategy and by establishing dual state regulatory functions, as described in chapter 8. With the operation and oversight of innovative schools separated from the traditional, the regulation and management functions that work best for each sector can be keyed in.

Professionals may choose whether or not they would like to enter into the work on innovation. Those in the traditional sector will have every incentive to see those schools do as well as they can. For those at work on innovation, enrollment will be linked directly to the quality and appeal of their programs.

The key to making this arrangement work is the codification of a sound system, including set rules, light regulation, and fair play. As some schools see stronger enrollment than others, there will be political temptation to protect those that are less successful. This must be resisted.

Problem: Teacher unions oppose change.
Solution: Show them how to become drivers of change.

The topic of teacher unions and education reform may be the area where the largest number of otherwise good-thinking people lose the most clarity, the quickest. Emotions win out.

There are basically two ways to address the unions' historical resistance to change. One is to attempt to blow up the unions by fiat (although nobody seems to know how this would be done), or wait until the spread of nonunionized alternatives such as chartering erode their base of membership. Neither of these is particularly appealing, as the former is not politically viable and the latter would be slow and chaotic.

The character of teacher unions is commonly misunderstood. First and foremost, in present form they are a function of the system. They are a system effect, and so change will not come from targeting the behavior of the people but by figuring out and addressing what causes it.

The behaviors that can be observed—the obsession over credentialing, the use of the blunt collective bargaining mechanism over individual contract negotiation, the resistance to change—are rational and predictable responses to the very real plight of the teacher.

Teaching in a traditional public school resembles a blue-collar job. And a blue-collar job begets a blue-collar union—a labor union. What critics seem to be agitating for is for the unions to behave more like white-collar professional associations, where the interests of the clients and quality of practice are put first. The problem is that teaching in many ways is not a white-collar job, and teachers are not treated as white-collar professionals. So we should not expect them to behave as such.

As long as teachers are denied basic professional controls, collective bargaining and collective protection will be the most effective way for them to exercise influence. The labor union will be the vehicle. But as alternative governance models develop that provide teachers with greater degrees of control over their work and environment, teachers will find they do not need these types of labor protections.

This presents a remarkable opportunity for the unions to expand their scope, and to begin working to improve the lot of their members. They can do this not by demanding more from the bosses, but by giving their members more and more control, effectively making *teachers* the bosses.

This could get unions out of the corner they have painted themselves into, as the organizations of "no." Already many local union chapters and some national leaders are moving toward this in Boston, Los Angeles, Denver, and Minneapolis. Teachers are recognizing an opportunity to take control of it by stepping forward and running schools themselves. Lawyers do it. Doctors do it. So do architects. Why not teachers?

Problem: Everyone cannot agree about what to do.
Solution: Provide opportunities—do not compel.

"Not everyone agrees" is an excuse often cited for inaction. The fact is that there will never be agreement on which types of new schools to create, what pedagogy to use, and which subjects should be taught and how. Consensus is not possible, because people are different.

Instead of seeking a couple of best practices to bring to scale, policymakers should let demand inform the development of schools. Student and their family choice is a legitimate proxy for quality. They seek safe, strong, healthy schools, and through force of enrollment they can hold schools to a standard that regulators could never hope to impose.

To make this possible, state regulatory bodies should continue moving from administering uniformity to overseeing plurality. The state and federal governments need to lighten their narrow definitions of what counts as learning.

Students should not be made to attend a school they do not wish to, and those who want models and expanded ways to demonstrate learning should have them available.

Problem: Standards make schools teach to government tests.
Solution: Expand our definition of achievement.

Universal standards will be either universally low or generally thwarted. This was observed during the enactment of No Child Left Behind when states, understanding the political cost of widespread failure of students to meet state standards, chose to set the bar so low that few did. It is clear that students do not learn from standards alone, and if they are lowered so schools are not compelled to change then their desired effect is lost.

Innovation requires a wider definition of what counts as achievement in learning. By including more types of learning in what government considers legitimate, the likelihood of students identifying with and being motivated by a particular learning model increases.

Students excel in different ways—some in math, some in literature, some in arts; some through lecture, some through project-based learning, some with self-study. Regulation, oversight, and evaluation must be able to accommodate the extraordinary.

The common standards approach risks ignoring the extraordinary by focusing on a common denominator with particular subject areas. Do not confuse the importance of high expectations in practice with the placing of common standards on paper. (See figure 9.1.)

Problem: We need better teachers.
Solution: Make teaching a better job.

The inability of public education to attract enough highly talented professionals is perhaps the greatest challenge facing the system. To attract

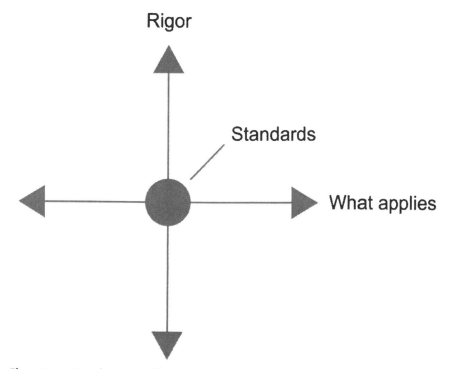

Figure 9.1. Introduce variability to content standards

top-tier college graduates, innovative and entrepreneurial college graduates, or mid-career transfers, teaching has to be made a better job. Fundamentally, this is not a problem of pay or prestige. Teaching in traditional schools and in the district arrangement too often feels like a blue-collar job. Highly capable young people with the world at their fingertips will not choose to work in a blue-collar job.

The prestige of teaching is reflective of the character of the job. Most teachers have very little actual authority in schools, and they have limited say in what is taught or how. So while teachers perform a vital public function, teaching is not commonly viewed with the same prestige as other fields such as medicine, law, or business.

The fact that teaching runs a labor-union model instead of a professional association model does not help its image. Here too, the union illustrates the nature of the job. If teachers had real authority over their work, if they had power inherent in their position in the system, then their unions would not need and would not have pay and work conditions as a primary focus.

Increase the professionalism of teaching. Give teachers greater degrees of control over their practice, including the functions of their schools. Tell them what needs to be done, not how to do it. Let the professionals hire the management. Administrators should work for the teachers, not the other way around. The more new schools move in this direction, the more they are showing that the appeal of the job can increase.

Problem: Kids just do not care nowadays.
Solution: Target motivation and treat them better—like adults.

There is a dichotomy that just does not make sense: Young people today are living in an age where electronic information is ubiquitous, yet they attend schools where electronics are largely prohibited. Everything in their lives is differentiated by pace, content, degree. Yet education is uniform.

Motivation is central to learning, because effort helps determine performance. Students are sat in desks, told to be quiet and behave, and to take what is given to them—with no regard for their interests, capacities, or passions. Their electronics are prohibited. Students are treated as children.

Is it any wonder that they behave as they do? Treating people who are essentially adults as kids is fraught with problems. In urban areas, where people often assume very adult responsibilities by their early teens, this arrangement is a nonstarter. Any reform efforts that continue with a school model that treats students like children, especially in urban areas, will face an uphill climb.

Instead, as with teachers, give students greater control over their work. Let them choose the pace, content, and style of their learning. Give them a choice of many different kinds of schools. Design models of school that use technology in ways that are more reflective of the real world.

Schools will find that students are actually quite passionate about learning and are doing it every day. Many of us just do not recognize it.

Problem: Parents are wary of change.
Solution: Start with the "nonconsumers."

The greatest resistance to change will come from parents who either do not trust a new idea or are satisfied with and want to maintain their student's present arrangement. This reemphasizes the need to run a split-screen strategy for improvement, making change possible and optional but never required.

Christensen recommends deploying new technologies first for non-consumers, or those for whom there is not presently an option. Home-schooled or rural students will be more likely to try innovative Web-based programs than those who can take it in their school — because for them the alternative is nothing at all.

Students in schools who are cutting courses not core to government requirements — languages, AP, specialty subjects — may find it more desirable to take some time out of the classroom to go into a virtual space and take the classes. Here, too, the alternative is nothing at all, so the students and parents are grateful for the opportunity.

As the new and different ways of doing things (new technologies, new school models) progress and improve in quality, their appeal will grow and others may choose them who would not in the beginning

Problem: In decline, rural districts are going through painful consolidation.
Solution: Rethink it. Combine new technologies with new school models and shared services.

Consolidation is a popular practice for rural school districts facing budget challenges. Similarly, there is a movement by districts to run on four-day weeks, by extending the school days.

Neither of these policies is a long-term solution. Understand that consolidation is not a strategy to address cost drivers. The strategy of consolidation is based on the idea that to reach an economy of scale there must be one large school. That is no longer the case. Districts may form cooperatives to share services or specialty staff. Courses without sufficient demand to hire a teacher can be contracted for, online. Technology can be used to bring in specialized content, perform a tutoring function, and connect students throughout the world.

There is some truth to the notion that size breeds cost. The larger a school becomes, the farther students must travel to get there. Relationships break down, and so specialists are hired. Decorum slides. Any number of maladies arises, drawing down resources and distracting attention from what is really important.

As rural schools get creative they start to see that technology is actually presenting them with a renaissance. They may remain local, because the virtual world can provide necessary services on a small scale. The large, comprehensive high school is now a choice, not a necessity.

Problem: Buying more IT is just not possible when money is tight.
Solution: Show how technology will improve productivity and leverage the savings.

Many uses of electronics in schools are not cost saving and do not significantly improve productivity. Technological literacy is important, but it is becoming more difficult politically to justify increases in spending without returns on performance.

Where new technologies can be shown to remake school for the better, and not simply an add-on, resources will come. When innovation in school models catches up with advances made in electronics, excitement will build.

Beyond this, there are two challenges in the financing of IT: the initial capital cost and the tail of training, operating, and maintenance.

Methods for covering the initial outlay may include rerouting general operating funds, floating bonds, raising private donations and grants, or holding a referendum and seeking other one-time public grants.

To finance the maintenance and operation costs, schools and districts may set up independent foundations, raise money through taxes, or try to grow their general operational funds by increasing enrollment.

There is another way as well: financing improvements with savings rather than with new money. The real reduction in costs happens when schools move away from the expensive and inefficient factory model and get into a mode where they are operating more efficiently.

Put this into the realm of value. Private philanthropies and the public will be more willing to provide the initial capital for technology if they see it as improving the value of school. This means either cutting costs without decreasing quality, or significantly increasing performance for the same price.

Termination

Make It Possible to Graduate Early

Many young people, if provided the opportunity, information, and encouragement, would jump at the opportunity to graduate high school one or two years ahead of schedule.

Legislatures can make it possible for students to take college courses while in high school, or to graduate early upon demonstration of competence. Another strategy could be allowing students to test-out of K–12 by testing in to postsecondary. A shift from exit requirements to entry requirements properly aligns incentives and works to maximize student motivation.

States could see 5, 10, or 20 percent of their young people finishing high school and college in six years instead of eight—with tremendous savings and two more years of productivity for the economy. The state can encourage this by splitting the savings with students in the form of rebating taxes or college debt. At $10,000 per student per year, the potential savings accumulate quickly.

Notes

1. K. Insley, May 20, 2010. www.kare11.com/life/community/schools/education/education_article.aspx?storyid=851280&catid=213. Retrieved from Expert: Minn. "Will Have Long-term Problems Funding Education."

2. Naomi Stanford. The Economist *Guide to Organisation Design*. London: Profile Books, 2007.

3. Bagehot, Walter. *Physics and Politics*. Gloucestershire, England: Dodo Press, 2006.

4. Clayton, Horn, and Johnson. *Distrupting Class*.

5. Tim McDonald and Ted Kolderie. "The Role of Information Technology in Creating New Kinds of American High Schools." Information Technology and Innovation Foundation. 2009. www.itif.org/files/Education_ITIF.pdf.

6. Robert Greene. *The 33 Strategies of War*. New York: Viking, 2006.

7. Bagehot. *Physics and Politics*.

8. John Brandl and Vin Weber, eds. "An Agenda for Reform: Competition, Community, Concentration, Minnesota. 1995."

9. Conversation during a Minnesota House/Senate conference committee, May 22, 2009; speakers are representatives Pat Garofalo (R) and Mindy Greiling (D).

10. Civic Caucus. "Summary of Discussion with Ron Johnson." August 7, 2010. www.civiccaucus.org.

11. Paul Hill and Marguerite Roza. "Curing Baumol's Disease: In Search of Productivity Gains in K–12 Schooling." Center on Reinventing Public Education (CRPE). July 22, 2010. www.crpe.org/cs/crpe/view/csr_pubs/343.

12. EducationlEvolving. "Clayton Christensen Speaks on 'Disruptive Innovation' in Education, 2005." http://www.educationevolving.org/clayton-christensen-speech-2005.

13. Minnesota Office of Management and Budget, and Budget Trends Study Commission: Report to the Legislature, State of Minnesota. 2009.

14. U.S. Department of Education. "A Test of Leadership: Charting the Future of U.S. Higher Education." 2006. www.ed.gov/about/bdscomm/list/hiedfuture/reports/final-report.pdf.

15. Per-student expenditures determined by total expenditures in 2009 divided by total reported enrollment.

16. Carrie Bakken. "Teacher Voices on Video." www.educationevolving.org/teacherpartnerships/teacher_videos.

17. Larry Cuban. *Oversold and Underused: Computers in the Classroom.* Cambridge, MA: Harvard University Press, 2003.

18. Civic Caucus, February 19, 2010. "Larry Pogemiller, Senate Majority Leader." www.civiccaucus.org/Interviews/Pogemiller-Larry_02-12-10.htm.

19. Walter McClure, 1981. "Structure and Incentive Problems in Economic Regulation of Medical Care." Retrieved from www.bellagiovanna.com/files/McClure-Structure-and-Incentives-in-Health-Care.pdf.

20. William Ouchi. *The Secret of TSL.* New York: Simon & Schuster, 2010.

21. Clayton M. Christensen, Michael B. Horn, and Curtis W. Johnson. *Disrupting Class: How Disruptive Innovation Will Change the Way the World Learns.* New York: McGraw Hill, 2008.

22. Steve Hargadon, Interview with Michael Horn. September 17, 2009. http://www.futureofeducation.com/.

23. C. S. Lewis. *Mere Christianity.* New York: HarperOne, 2001.

24. Walt McClure. "Unconventional Wisdom." January 1994. www.bellagiovanna.com/files/McClure-Unconventional-Wisdom.pdf.

25. "Project Tomorrow Reports on Technology." www.tomorrow.org/speakup/speakup_reports.html.

26. Peter Stanyer and Elroy Dimson. *Guide to Investment Strategy: How to Understand Markets, Risk, Rewards and Behavior (The Economist).* New York: Bloomberg Press, 2006.

27. Ted Kolderie et al. "The Other Half of the Strategy." Education|Evolving, n.d. www.educationevolving.org/pdf/Innovatingwithschooling.pdf.

28. Clayton, Horn, and Johnson. *Distrupting Class.*

Bibliography

ARTICLES

American College Testing Program (ACT). "2006 ACT National Score Report News Release." August 16, 2006. www.act.org/news/releases/2006/ndr.html (accessed July 13, 2009).

Ash, Katie. "Crafting a New Generation of Assessments." *Education Week: Digital Directions.* February 2009. www.edweek.org/dd/articles/2009/02/17/04ddassessment.h02.html.

Baer, Justin D., Andrea L. Cook, and Stéphane Baldi. "The Literacy of America's College Students," American Institutes for Research. January 2006. www.air.org/news/documents/The%20Literacy%20of%20Americas%20College%20Students_final%20report.pdf.

Becker, Stacy. *Education Finance: More Money or Different Spending Choices. What Factors Make a Difference?* Education|Evolving. 2005. www.educationevolving.org/pdf/Education_Finance.pdf.

Borsuk, Alan J. "MPS to Explore Dissolving District." *Milwaukee Journal Sentinel,* September 18, 2008.

Brandl, John E. "Politics and Policy in Minnesota." *Daedalus* 129, Summer 2000.

Broede, Jim. "Teachers Propose Eliminating 31 Jobs to Improve Their Pay in Forest Lake." *St. Paul Pioneer Press,* June 25, 1991.

Center for Research on Education Outcomes, Stanford University (CREDO). *Multiple Choice: Charter School Performance in 16 States.* 2009. credo.stanford.edu/reports/MULTIPLE_CHOICE_CREDO.pdf.

Christensen, Clayton M., Sally Aaron, and William Clark. "Can Schools Improve?" *Phi Delta Kappan,* March 2005, 545–550.

Chubb, John, Terry Moe, and Larry Cuban. "Will Education Technology Change the Role of the Teacher and the Nature of Learning?" *Education Next* 9, no. 1 (2009).

Civic Caucus. "Different Choices: Redesigning Public Services." December 16, 2009. www.civiccaucus.org/Report_Redesign_12-16-09.htm.

———. "Summary of Discussion with Ted Kolderie and Joe Graba." April 30, 2010. www.civiccaucus.org/.

Fletcher, J. D. "Technology, the Columbus Effect, and the Third Revolution in Learning." Institute for Defense Analyses, April 2001. www.eric.ed.gov:80/ERICWebPortal/custom/portlets/recordDetails/detailmini.jsp?_nfpb=true&_&ERICExtSearch_SearchValue_0=ED474406&ERICExtSearch_SearchType_0=no&accno=ED474406.

Fletcher, J .D., Sigmund Tobias, and Robert A. Wisher. "Learning Anytime, Anywhere: Advanced Distributed Learning and the Changing Face of Education." *Educational Researcher* 36, no. 2 (2007):96–102.

Gao, Guodong, and Lorin M. Hitt. "Information Technology and Product Variety: Evidence from Panel Data." 25th International Conference on Information Systems, Washington, D.C., December 12–15, 2004. opim.wharton.upenn.edu/~lhitt/files/itvariety.pdf.

Hein, George E. "Constructivist Learning Theory." CECA (International Committee of Museum Educators) Conference, Jerusalem, October 15–22, 1991. www.exploratorium.edu/IFI/resources/constructivistlearning.html.

Hill, Paul. "Performance Management in Portfolio School Districts." Center on Reinventing Public Education. August 2009. www.crpe.org/cs/crpe/download/csr_files/pub_dscr_portfperf_aug09.pdf.

Hill, Paul, Marguerite Roza, and James Harvey. "Facing the Future: Financing Productive Schools." Center on Reinventing Public Education. 2008. www.crpe.org/cs/crpe/download/csr_files/pub_sfrp_finalrep_nov08.pdf.

"Historical Annual Financial Investment Framework: $90.0 M." A report to the Minnesota Legislature. University of Minnesota, 2009.

Johnson, Diane C. Educational Reform: Bringing Efficiency to Schools. Stanford University, 1984.

Kain, E. D. "The Education Bailout." New Majority, October 8, 2009.

Kolderie, Ted. "First Thoughts on Sustainability and Productivity." Education| Evolving, n.d. www.educationevolving.org/pdf/Sustainability_and_Productivity.pdf.

———. "Growing Advances in Digital Electronics." Education|Evolving, n.d. www.educationevolving.net/pdf/Advances_in_digital_electronics.pdf.

———. "Sparking Greater Innovation in K–12 Education." Transcript of webinar on Education Week, March 26, 2008. www.edweek.org/chat/transcript_03_26_08.html?r=444430151.

———. 2009. "What Are the 'Other Ways' of Doing Things? Alternatives, and How They're Installed."

[handwritten annotation] Who is he? None appears peer-reviewed.

———. "What Do We Do—on the Spending Side?" Talk to Minnesota Taxpayers Association Annual Meeting, Saint Paul, MN. 2009.

———. "What Do We Mean by 'Privatization'?" *Society* 24, no. 6 (1987):46–51.

Lerman, Steven R. "Some Criteria for the Evaluation of Multimedia Computer Applications." In *School Improvement through Media in Education*, 67 (1995). Gütersloh, Germany: Bertelsmann Foundation.

Levine, Arthur E. "Waiting for the Transformation." *Education Week*, February 25, 2009. www.edweek.org/login.html?source=http://www.edweek.org/ew/articles/2009/02/25/22levine_ep.h28.html&destination=http://www.edweek.org/ew/articles/2009/02/25/22levine_ep.h28.html&levelId=2100.

Lips, Dan, Shanea Watkins, and John Fleming. "Does Spending More on Education Improve Academic Achievement?" Heritage Foundation Backgrounder 2179, September 8, 2008. www.heritage.org/research/Education/bg2179.cfm (accessed July 13, 2009).

Madkour, Rasha. "Need Help with Class? YouTube Videos Await." Associated Press, December 11, 2008. www.msnbc.msn.com/id/28200197/.

McClure, Walter. "Structure and Incentive Problems in Economic Regulation of Medical Care." *Health and Society* 59, no. 2 (1981):107–144.

McDonald, Tim. "Rethinking the Student-Centered Classroom." Engage Learner, August 12, 2008. www.engagelearner.org/index.php?option=com_content&view=article&id=48:rethinking-the-student-centered-classroom&catid=36:k-12-policy&Itemid=60.

Means, Barbara, et al. *Evaluation of Evidence-Based Practices in Online Learning: A Meta-Analysis and Review of Online Learning Studies*. Washington, DC: U.S. Department of Education, 2009. www2.ed.gov/rschstat/eval/tech/evidence-based-practices/finalreport.pdf.

Minnesota Office of Management and Budget. "Total State 2010–11 Operating Budget." February 2010. www.mmb.state.mn.us/doc/budget/report-pie/all-feb10.pdf.

"MPS Financial Facts and Student Achievement." Minneapolis Public Schools. www.mpls.k12.mn.us/mps_financial_facts.html.

National Commission on Excellence in Education. "A Nation at Risk: The Imperative for Educational Reform, 1983." U.S. Department of Education, April 1983. www.ed.gov/pubs/NatAtRisk/index.html.

Odden, Allan. "Fifteen Years of 'CPRE's School Finance Research." Education|Evolving. www.educationevolving.org/pdf/CPRE_School-Finance_Research.pdf.

Organization for Economic Co-operation and Development (OECD). *Learning for Tomorrow's World: First Results from PISA 2003*. 2004. www.oecd.org/document/55/0,3343,en_32252351_32236173_33917303_1_1_1_1,00.html.

Pitzl, Mary Jo. "GOP Budget Plan Slashes Funds for Arizona Education." *Arizona Republic*, January 16, 2009. www.azcentral.com/arizonarepublic/news/articles/2009/01/16/20090116capitol-budget0116.html.

Rae-Dupree, Janet. "Disruptive Innovation, Applied to Health Care." *New York Times*, February 1, 2009. www.nytimes.com/2009/02/01/business/01unbox.html.

Roza, Marguerite. "Projections of State Budget Shortfalls on K–12 Public Education Spending and Job Loss." Center on Reinventing Public Education (CRPE). February 9, 2009. www.crpe.org/cs/crpe/download/csr_files/rr_crpe_shortfall_feb09.pdf.

Roza, Marguerite, Kacey Guin, and Tricia Davis. "What Is the Sum of the Parts?" Center on Reinventing Public Education (CRPE). 2008. www.crpe.org/cs/crpe/download/csr_files/pub_sfrp_weights_jun08.pdf.

Russell Chaddock, Gail. "U.S. High School Dropout Rate: High, but How High?" *Christian Science Monitor*, June 21, 2006. www.csmonitor.com/2006/0621/p03s02-ussc.html (accessed July 13, 2009).

Sanders, Jim. "Schwarzenegger Seeks Education Cuts." *Sacramento Bee*, January 1, 2009.

Trotter, Andrew. "Mobile Devices Seen as Key to 21st-Century Learning." *Education Week*, January 9, 2009. www.edweek.org/dd/articles/2009/01/09/04mobile.h02.html.

"Where the Axe Should Fall." *The Economist*, September 26, 2009.

Whitehurst, Grover. "Innovation, Motherhood, and Apple Pie." *Brown Center Letters on Education*, 2009. www.brookings.edu/~/media/Files/rc/papers/2009/0319_innovation_whitehurst/03_innovation_whitehurst.pdf.

Whitmire, Richard M., and Andrew Rotherham. "How Teacher Unions Lost the Media." *Wall Street Journal*, October 1, 2009. online.wsj.com/article/SB10001424052970204488304574426991456414888.html.

Wooldridge, Adrian. "The World Turned Upside Down: A Special Report on Innovation in Emerging Markets." *The Economist*, April 17, 2010.

Young, George P. "Electronics Technology for Public School Systems: A Superintendent's View." 1981. *Educational Technology*.

BOOKS

Berkun, Scott. *The Myths of Innovation*. Sebastopol, CA: O'Reilly Media, 2007.

Christensen, Clayton M. *The Innovator's Dilemma: When New Technologies Cause Great Firms to Fail*. Boston, MA: Harvard Business School Press, 1997.

Christensen, Clayton M., Jerome H. Grossman, and Jason Hwang. *The Innovator's Prescription: A Disruptive Solution for Health Care*. New York: McGraw Hill, 2009.

Dirkswager, Edward (ed.). *Teachers as Owners*. Lanham, MD: Scarecrow Press, 2002.

Downes, Larry. *The Laws of Disruption: Harnessing the New Forces That Govern Life and Business in the Digital Age*. New York: Basic Books, 2009.

Epstein, Robert. *The Case against Adolescence*. Sanger, CA: Quill Driver Books, 2007.

Greene, Robert. *The 48 Laws of Power*. London: Profile Books, 1998.

Hanushek, Erik A., and Alfred A. Lindseth. *Schoolhouses, Courthouses, and Statehouses*. Princeton, NJ: Princeton University Press, 2009.

Ingersoll, Richard M. *Who Controls Teachers' Work?* Cambridge, MA: Harvard University Press, 2003.

Kolderie, Ted. *Creating the Capacity for Change: How and Why Governors and Legislatures Are Opening a New-Schools Sector in Public Education*. 2nd ed. Bethesda, MD: Education Week Press, 2004.

Maddux, Cleborne D., and D. LaMont Johnson. *Classroom Integration of Type II Uses of Technology in Education*. New York: Haworth Press, 2005.

——. *Internet Applications of Type II Uses of Technology in Education*. New York: Haworth Press, 2005.

Maddux, Cleborne D., and D. LaMont Johnson (eds). *Type II Uses of Technology in Education: Projects, Case Studies, and Software Applications*. New York: Haworth Press, 2006.

Moe, Terry, and John Chubb. *Liberating Learning: Technology, Politics, and the Future of American Education*. San Francisco: Jossey-Bass, 2009.

Monnet, Jean. *Memoirs*. Garden City, NY: Doubleday, 1978.

Roza, Marguerite. *Educational Economics: Where Do School Funds Go?* Washington, DC: Urban Institute Press, 2010.

Schall, James. *The Order of Things*. San Francisco: Ignatius Press, 2007.

Taleb, Nassim N. *The Black Swan: The Impact of the Highly Improbable*. New York: Random House, 2007.

Thomas, Doug, Walter Enloe, and Ron Newell, eds. *"The Coolest School in America."* Lanham, MD: Scarecrow Education, 2005.

Zucker, Andrew. *Transforming Schools with Technology: How Smart Use of Digital Tools Helps Achieve Six Key Education Goals*. Cambridge, MA: Harvard Education Press, 2008.

About the Author

Tim McDonald is a fellow at the Center for Policy Studies in the United States, and an associate with EducationIEvolving. The content of this book and the ideas it puts forth are a cooperative effort including members of EducationIEvolving, the Center for Policy Studies, and many associated colleagues. EducationIEvolving is a Minnesota-based policy group committed to system reform to help public schooling change and meet the challenges, demands, and opportunities of the 21st century. Follow their blog at www.EducationInnovating.org, visit EIE online at www.Education Evolving.org, and visit Tim online at www.BellaGiovanna.com.